STATEMENTS: THREE PLAYS

Also by
ATHOL FUGARD

Dimetos and Two Early Plays
(Dimetos, No-good Friday, and Nongogo)

Boesman and Lena and Other Plays
(The Blood Knot, People Are Living There, Hello and Goodbye,
and *Boesman and Lena)*

A Lesson from Aloes

'Master Harold' . . . **and the boys**

ATHOL FUGARD

STATEMENTS

Two Workshop Productions
devised by Athol Fugard, John Kani, and
Winston Ntshona

SIZWE BANSI IS DEAD
AND
THE ISLAND

and

STATEMENTS AFTER AN ARREST
UNDER THE IMMORALITY ACT

Oxford   New York
OXFORD UNIVERSITY PRESS

Oxford University Press, Walton Street, Oxford OX2 6DP

Oxford New York Toronto
Delhi Bombay Calcutta Madras Karachi
Kuala Lumpur Singapore Hong Kong Tokyo
Nairobi Dar es Salaam Cape Town
Melbourne Auckland

and associated companies in
Beirut Berlin Ibadan Mexico City Nicosia

Oxford is a trade mark of Oxford University Press

ISBN 0–19–281170–3

First published 1974
Sixth impression 1985

Made and Printed in Great Britain by
The Guernsey Press Co. Ltd., Guernsey, Channel Islands.

CONTENTS

INTRODUCTION

Thirteen years ago, in an introductory note to a published extract from my play *The Blood Knot*, I put down a few thoughts about what I called 'the pure theatre experience'. I wrote:

> 'This experience belongs to the audience. He is my major concern as a playwright. The ingredients of this experience are already partially revealed in what I have said and are very simple—their very simplicity being the main justification for using the word "pure" in the context of a form as open to adulteration as Theatre. They are: the actor and the stage, the actor *on* the stage. Around him is space, to be filled and defined by movement and gesture; around him is also silence to be filled with meaning, using words and sounds, and at moments when all else fails him, including the words, the silence itself.'

I concluded:

> 'In other words the full and unique possibility of this experience needs nothing more than the actor and the stage, the actor in space and silence. Externals, and in a sense even the text can be one, will profit nothing if the actor has no soul.'

There is obviously no credit attached to recognizing Theatre's fundamental dependence on the actor. What I do recognize now, however, in those few lines I wrote thirteen years ago, is the first formulation of an obsessional concern with the actor and his performance. This has been a major factor in my work, certainly to the extent that if it is categorized at all, then it must be as 'actors' theatre'. Without this primary involvement with the actor I would never have ended up 'making' theatre with them as I did thirteen years later with the three plays in this volume. It is partly for this reason also that I have directed most of my plays in thier first productions; not because I felt that as the author I was in possession of *the* interpretation either of the play as a whole or the specific characters, but because I have always regarded the completed text as being only a half-way stage to my ultimate objective—the living performance and its particular definition of space and silence.

The next of the developments which led finally to the three plays in this volume came about as a result of my association with Serpent Players, the African drama group from New Brighton, Port Elizabeth. Seven years ago, after being in existence for four years (during which, among other plays, we performed *Antigone*) we decided to experiment with improvised theatre. Our reason for this was quite simply the desire to use the stage for a much more immediate and direct relationship with our audience than had been possible with the 'ready-made' plays we had been doing. Our first attempt was a sixty-minute exercise called *The Coat* and was based on an actual incident. The coat in questioned belonged to a New Brighton man, one of many, who had been found guilty of membership of a banned political organization and sentenced to five years imprisonment. It was all he had to send back to his wife. In an interview I have described the evolution of the exercise as follows:

'First we just wanted to see the moment when the coat was handed over. So we very crudely, using almost no words, improvised that one scene—the coat leaving Mabel's hands and ending up in the wife's. Nothing more. Just the coat being handed over. Then we asked: "What do you do with the coat now that you've got it?" The wife, the actress playing the wife, said: "Well, I'm in my house. I've now heard about my husband. I know I'm not going to see him for five years. I've got his coat in my hands. I'll hang it up, first of all, and then go on working. I want to think about him. And the coat." She was a good actress and in the course of all this, something happened. It took a few exercises to fatten it. Know what I mean?

'I jotted down, very crudely, several of her attempts and at the end we compared notes. I said: "This is how the last one came out, Nomhle." The other actors joined in: "Yes, that's right. You did. And remember that other thing she said when she was talking about the street? I thought that was rather good." I made a few more notes and handed them over to her. "Take these away. Come back next week. Same time, same place. Live with them. See if you can fill them out a bit."

'She did. Next week we provoked her again and that little scene and its follow-up seemed intact. It had a shape, a life of its own. Then we provoked her still further, by questions and discussing, and in this way it all started to grow.

'I remember! At one stage we were trying to corner her. We felt that a certain edge of desperation in the wife's predicament was still eluding her. We said to Humphrey: "Come on. We need a scene with the man at the Rent Office to whom she is going to appeal for a few days' grace. Will you take it on?" He did. The two of them discussed the "geography" of the little encounter for a second or so and then tried it out. That one almost worked completely the first time. In all of this I acted as scribe . . . you know, making my little notes and keeping an eye on the overall structure . . . .'

The Coat was followed by many similar experiments over the next few years. I am enormously indebted to them, but equivalently I must admit that looking back now I am very conscious of them as being two-dimensional. Facts, and somehow we never managed to get beyond facts even though they were important facts, are flat and lacking in the density and ambiguity of truly dramatic images. The reason for this limitation was that I relied exclusively on improvisation in its shallowest sense. I had not yet thought seriously about alternative methods of releasing the creative potential of the actor. This came with my reading of Grotowski a few years later, an encounter which coincided with a crisis in relation to my own work. For several years, and particularly as a writer, I had become increasingly dissatisfied with the type of Theatre I was making. The content and personal significance of my response to Grotowski's ideas—I have never seen an actual performance —are indicated in the following extracts from an interview in London three years ago:

'After the last run of *Boesman and Lena* in South Africa I decided to try and do something which had been on my mind for a long time. In a sense it involved turning my back on my securities as a writer. I regard my involvement in theatre as being total in the sense that I both direct and write, and sometimes even act. I am not yet addicted to the privacy of myself and blank paper to the exclusion of all else. I really do think I write plays because what I want ultimately is to be involved with actors and a living experience of the theatre. So, as I say, after that run of *Boesman and Lena* I decided to do something I had wanted to for a long time . . . turn my back on my securities, which is to write a play in total privacy, to go into a rehearsal room with a *completed* text which I would then take on as a director, and which the actors—under my direction—would go on to "illustrate", to use Grotowski's phrase.

'I mention Grotowski, because he was in every sense the *agent provocateur* at that moment in my career. His book *Towards a Poor Theatre* made me realize that there were other ways of doing theatre, other ways of creating a totally valid theatre experience . . . that it needn't be the orthodox experience I had been retailing for so many years since *The Blook Knot* . . . .

'My work had been so conventional! It involved the *writing* of a play; it involved *setting* that play in terms of local specifics; it involved the actors *assuming* false identities . . . etc., etc. I wanted to turn my back on all that. Permanently or not I didn't know. I just knew I wanted to be free again. I had an idea involving an incident in our recent South African history . . . a young man took a bomb into the Johannesburg station concourse as an act of protest. It killed an old woman. He was eventually caught and hanged. I superimposed, almost in the sense of a palimpsest, this image on that of Clytemnestra and her two children, Orestes and Electra. There was no text. Not a single piece of paper passed between myself and the actors. Three of them. Anyway, after about twelve weeks of totally private rehearsals we got around to what we called our first "exposure". This was an experience that lasted for sixty minutes, had about 300 words, a lot of action—strange, almost somnambulistic action—and silence. It was called *Orestes* . . . .

'What was so marvellous in working on this project, along lines suggested by Grotowski and my own experience, was just how pristine, what weight you gave to a line, a word, a gesture, if you set it in silence. . . .'

The only fact I do not find reflected in the above quotations was my total response to Grotowski's sense of the actor as a 'creative' artist, not merely 'interpretive'.

Orestes was my first, and remains my most extreme excursion into a new type of theatre experience, in which we attempted to communicate with our audience on the basis of, for us at least, an entirely new vocabulary. It has defied translation onto paper in any conventional sense. I have tried. At the moment it is 'scored' in three large drawing-books. It is one of the most important experiences I have had in Theatre and I will be living with it, and using it, for as long as I continue to work. I can think of no aspect of my work, either as writer or director, that it has not influenced.

In relation to the three plays in this volume the importance of *Orestes* was to suggest techniques for releasing the creative potential of the actor. But I would just like to make one point clear: we did not jettison the writer. It was never a question of coming together with the actors on a 'let's make a play' basis. The starting-point to our work was always at least an image, sometimes an already structured complex of images about which I, as a writer, was obsessional. In all three of these plays the writer provided us with a mandate in terms of which the actors then went on to work. In the case of *Sizwe Bansi* our starting-point was my fascination with a studio photograph I had once seen of a man with a cigarette in one hand and a pipe in the other; *The Island* began with the notes and ideas I had accumulated over many years relating to Robben Island; *Statements* likewise started with my image of six police photographs of a White woman and a Coloured man caught in the act of love-making.

These initial mandates from the writer were also not his final contribution. He kept pace with us as fast as we discovered and explored . . . sometimes as no more than a scribe, but at other times in a much more decisive way. The final dramatic structure of each play, for example, was his responsibility. Looking back on the three experiences now, it was as if instead of first putting words on paper in order to arrive eventually at the stage and a live performance, I was able to write *directly* into its space and silence via the actor.

In this context my dependence on the actor (and his ability to rise to the challenge involved) is even more fundamental than in the sense I showed at the beginning of these notes. I have made many attempts to formulate this challenge. A simple definition still eludes me, which I suppose is inevitable with an experience as obscure and at times as disturbing as those we have lived through in rehearsal rooms since *Orestes*. I do know, however, that it starts with—absolutely demands—a very special courage without which the actor cannot 'stake' his personal truth, and in the absence of words on paper that personal truth has been our only capital. I cannot stress this factor in strong enough terms. Pretence and deception are as fatal as they would be in a writer's private relationship with paper.

The basic device has been that of Challenge and Response. As writer-director I have challenged, and the actors have responded, not intellectually or merely verbally but with a totality of Being that at the risk of sounding pretentious I can only liken to a form of Zen spontaneity. As with the more obvious pitfalls of pretence and deception so too any element of calculation or premeditation in response has proved fatal. When, however, the response seemed meaningful in terms of the overall mandate provided by the writer, or to put it another way, when we thought it was of value and significance in terms of our intentions, we then applied ourselves to disciplining and structuring it so that the gesture, word, or event was capable of controlled repetition. I must stress this point. Spontaneous response and improvisation basically ended in the rehearsal room. Once the actor had created his text in the privacy of rehearsals, we then concerned ourselves with its performance in exactly the same way that we would have done with an independent text.

To arrive at an uninhibited release of Self is not easy. At times it has been painful. There have been harrowing experiences in rehearsal rooms. I say this without any sense of pride. It is just that in making these plays I have kept company with a group of remarkable actors. Their courage has at times frightened me. I have lived constantly with the fear of our work degenerating into a dangerous game with personalities. This might well be one of the reasons why at this point I feel that I have exhausted for myself personally the experience that started with *Orestes*, and that the time has now come to return to the privacy of blank paper.

I have included *Statements* in these notes although on the title page of this volume I claim sole authorship. The reason for this is that although I do regard myself as having *written* that play the production at the Royal Court Theatre, which this text partly reflects, was totally dependent on the methods I had evolved with *Orestes*.

Finally, one long overdue expression of gratitude. That is to Brian Astbury and his theatre The Space, in Cape Town. None of these plays would have happened if his vision and tenacity of purpose had not created that venue.

Athol Fugard
Skoenmakerskop
Port Elizabeth
March 1974

Quotations
(1) Foreword to *The Blood Knot* in *Contrast*, Vol. 2, No. 1.
(2) An interview with Athol Fugard about *The Coat* from *Two experiments in Play Making*, A. A. Balkema, Cape Town.
(3) Interview with Athol Fugard, from *Yale/Theatre*, Vol. 4, No. 1.

SIZWE BANSI IS DEAD

devised by

ATHOL FUGARD, JOHN KANI, AND WINSTON NTSHONA

CHARACTERS

STYLES
SIZWE BANSI
BUNTU

This play was given its first performance on 8 October 1972 at The Space, Cape Town, and was directed by Athol Fugard with the following cast:

Styles and Buntu	John Kani
Sizwe Bansi	Winston Ntshona

SIZWE BANSI IS DEAD

*Styles's Photographic Studio in the African township of New Brighton,
Port Elizabeth. Positioned prominently, the name-board:*

> *Styles Photographic Studio. Reference Books; Passports;
> Weddings; Engagements; Birthday Parties and Parties.*
>   *Prop.—Styles.*

*Underneath this a display of photographs of various sizes. Centre stage,
a table and chair. This is obviously used for photographs because a camera
on a tripod stands ready a short distance away.*

*There is also another table, or desk, with odds and ends of photographic
equipment and an assortment of 'props' for photographs.*

*The setting for this and subsequent scenes should be as simple as
possible so that the action can be continuous.*

*Styles walks on with a newspaper. A dapper, alert young man
wearing a white dustcoat and bowtie. He sits down at the table and starts
to read the paper.*

STYLES [*reading the headlines*]. 'Storm buffets Natal. Damage in
many areas . . . trees snapped like . . . what? . . . matchsticks. . . .'

[*He laughs.*]

They're having it, boy! And I'm watching it . . . in the paper.

[*Turning the page, another headline.*]

'China: A question-mark on South West Africa.' What's
China want there? *Yo!* They better be careful. China gets in
there . . . ! [*Laugh.*] I'll tell you what happens . . . .

[*Stops abruptly. Looks around as if someone might be eavesdropping on
his intimacy with the audience.*]

No comment.

[*Back to his paper.*]

What's this? . . . *Ag!* American politics. Nixon and all his
votes. Means buggerall to us.

[*Another page, another headline.*]

'Car plant expansion. 1·5 million rand plan.' *Ja.* I'll tell you
what *that* means . . . more machines, bigger buildings . . . never
any expansion to the pay-packet. Makes me fed-up. I know
what I'm talking about. I worked at Ford one time. We used

to read in the newspaper . . . big headlines! . . . 'So and so from America or London made a big speech: ". . . going to see to it that the conditions of their non-white workers in Southern Africa were substantially improved."' The talk ended in the bloody newspaper. Never in the pay-packet.

Another time we read: Mr Henry Ford Junior Number two or whatever the hell he is . . . is visiting the Ford Factories in South Africa!

[*Shakes his head ruefully at the memory.*]

Big news for us, man! When a big man like that visited the plant there was usually a few cents more in the pay-packet at the end of the week.

Ja, a Thursday morning. I walked into the plant . . . 'Hey! What's this?' . . . Everything was quiet! Those big bloody machines that used to make so much noise made my head go around . . . ? Silent! Went to the notice-board and read: Mr Ford's visit today!

The one in charge of us . . . [*laugh*] hey! I remember him. General Foreman Mr 'Baas' Bradley. Good man that one, if you knew how to handle him . . . he called us all together:

[*Styles mimics Mr 'Baas' Bradley. A heavy Afrikaans accent.*]

'Listen, boys, don't go to work on the line. There is going to be a General Cleaning first.'

I used to like General Cleaning. Nothing specific, you know, little bit here, little bit there. But that day! Yessus . . . in came the big machines with hot water and brushes—sort of electric mop—and God alone knows what else. We started on the floors. The oil and dirt under the machines was thick, man. All the time the bosses were walking around watching us:

[*Slapping his hands together as he urges on the 'boys'.*]

'Come on, boys! It's got to be spotless! Big day for the plant!' Even the *big* boss, the one we only used to see lunch-times, walking to the canteen with a big cigar in his mouth and his hands in his pocket . . . that day? Sleeves rolled up, running around us:

'Come on! Spotless, my boys! Over there, John. . . .' I thought: What the hell is happening? It was beginning to feel like hard work, man. I'm telling you we cleaned that place—

spot-checked after fifteen minutes! . . . like you would have thought it had just been built.

First stage of General Cleaning finished. We started on the second. Mr 'Baas' Bradley came in with paint and brushes. I watched.

W—h—i—t—e   l—i—n—e

[*Mr 'Baas' Bradley paints a long white line on the floor.*]

What's this? Been here five years and I never seen a white line before. Then:

[*Mr 'Baas' Bradley at work with the paint-brush.*]

CAREFUL THIS SIDE. TOW MOTOR IN MOTION.

[*Styles laughs.*]

It was nice, man. Safety-precautions after six years. Then another gallon of paint.

Y—e—l—l—o—w   l—i—n—e—

NO SMOKING IN THIS AREA. DANGER!

Then another gallon:

G—r—e—e—n   l—i—n—e—

I noticed that that line cut off the roughcasting section, where we worked with the rough engine blocks as we got them from Iscor. Dangerous world that. Big machines! One mistake there and you're in trouble. I watched them and thought: What's going to happen here? When the green line was finished, down they went on the floor— Mr 'Baas' Bradley, the lot!— with a big green board, a little brush, and a tin of white paint. EYE PROTECTION AREA. Then my big moment:

'Styles!'

'Yes, sir!'

[*Mr 'Baas' Bradley's heavy Afrikaans accent*] 'What do you say in your language for this? Eye Protection Area.'

It was easy, man!

'*Gqokra Izi Khuselo Zamehlo Kule Ndawo.*'

Nobody wrote it!

'Don't bloody fool me, Styles!'

'No, sir!'

'Then spell it . . . slowly.'

[*Styles has a big laugh.*]

Hey! That was my moment, man. Kneeling there on the

floor . . . foreman, general foreman, plant supervisor, plant manager . . . and Styles? Standing!

[*Folds his arms as he acts out his part to the imaginary figures crouched on the floor.*]

'*G—q—o—k—r—a*' . . . and on I went, with Mr 'Baas' Bradley painting and saying as he wiped away the sweat: 'You're not fooling me, hey!'

After that the green board went up. We all stood and admired it. Plant was looking nice, man! Colourful!

Into the third phase of General Cleaning.

'Styles!'

'Yes, sir!'

'Tell all the boys they must now go to the bathroom and wash themselves clean.'

We needed it! Into the bathroom, under the showers . . . hot water, soap . . . on a Thursday! Before ten? *Yo!* What's happening in the plant? The other chaps asked me: What's going on, Styles? I told them: 'Big-shot cunt from America coming to visit you.' When we finished washing they gave us towels . . . [*laugh*].

Three hundred of us, man! We were so clean we felt shy! Stand there like little ladies in front of the mirror. From there to the General Store.

Handed in my dirty overall.

'Throw it on the floor.'

'Yes, sir!'

New overall comes, wrapped in plastic. Brand new, man! I normally take a thirty-eight but this one was a forty-two. Then next door to the tool room . . . brand new tool bag, set of spanners, shifting spanner, torque wrench—all of them brand new—and because I worked in the dangerous hot test section I was also given a new asbestos apron and fire-proof gloves to replace the ones I had lost about a year ago. I'm telling you I walked back heavy to my spot. Armstrong on the moon! Inside the plant it was general meeting again. General Foreman Mr 'Baas' Bradley called me.

'Styles!'

'Yes, sir.'

'Come translate.'

'Yes, sir!'

[*Styles pulls out a chair. Mr 'Baas' Bradley speaks on one side, Styles translates on the other.*]

'Tell the boys in your language, that this is a very big day in their lives.'

'Gentlemen, this old fool says this is a hell of a big day in our lives.'

The men laughed.

'They are very happy to hear that, sir.'

'Tell the boys that Mr Henry Ford the Second, the owner of this place, is going to visit us. Tell them Mr Ford is the big Baas. He owns the plant and everything in it.'

'Gentlemen, old Bradley says this Ford is a big bastard. He owns everything in this building, which means you as well.'

A voice came out of the crowd:

'Is he a bigger fool than Bradley?'

'They're asking, sir, is he bigger than you?'

'Certainly . . . [*blustering*] . . . certainly. He is a very big baas. He's a . . . [*groping for words*] . . . he's a Makulu Baas.'

I loved that one!

'Mr "Baas" Bradley says most certainly Mr Ford is bigger than him. In fact Mr Ford is the grandmother baas of them all . . . that's what he said to me.'

'Styles, tell the boys that when Mr Henry Ford comes into the plant I want them all to look happy. We will slow down the speed of the line so that they can sing and smile while they are working.'

'Gentlemen, he says that when the door opens and his grandmother walks in you must see to it that you are wearing a mask of smiles. Hide your true feelings, brothers. You must sing. The joyous songs of the days of old before we had fools like this one next to me to worry about.' [*To Bradley.*] 'Yes, sir!'

'Say to them, Styles, that they must try to impress Mr Henry Ford that they are better than those monkeys in his own country, those niggers in Harlem who know nothing but strike, strike.'

Yo! I liked that one too.

'Gentlemen, he says we must remember, when Mr Ford walks in, that we are South African monkeys, not American monkeys. South African monkeys are much better trained. . . .'

Before I could even finish, a voice was shouting out of the crowd:
'He's talking shit!' I had to be careful!
[*Servile and full of smiles as he turns back to Bradley.*]
'No, sir! The men say they are much too happy to behave like those American monkeys.'
Right! Line was switched on nice and slow—and we started working.
[*At work on the Assembly Line; singing.*]
'*Tshotsholoza . . . Tshotsholoza . . . kulezondawo. . . .*'
We had all the time in the world, man! . . . torque wrench out . . . tighten the cylinder-head nut . . . wait for the next one. . . . [*Singing*] '*Vyabaleka . . . vyabaleka . . . kulezondawo. . . .*'
I kept my eye on the front office. I could see them—Mr 'Baas' Bradley, the line supervisor—through the big glass window, brushing their hair, straightening the tie. There was some General Cleaning going on there too.
[*He laughs.*]
We were watching them. Nobody was watching us. Even the old Security Guard. The one who every time he saw a black man walk past with his hands in his pockets he saw another spark-plug walk out of the plant. Today? To hell and gone there on the other side polishing his black shoes.
Then, through the window, I saw three long black Galaxies zoom up. I passed the word down the line: He's come!
Let me tell you what happened. The big doors opened; next thing the General Superintendent, Line Supervisor, General Foreman, Manager, Senior Manager, Managing Director . . . the bloody lot were there . . . like a pack of puppies!
[*Mimics a lot of fawning men retreating before an important person.*]
I looked and laughed! 'Yessus, Styles, they're all playing your part today!' They ran, man! In came a tall man, six foot six, hefty, full of respect and dignity . . . I marvelled at him! Let me show you what he did.
[*Three enormous strides*] One . . . two . . . three. . . . [*Cursory look around as he turns and takes the same three strides back.*]
One . . . two . . . three . . . OUT! Into the Galaxie and gone! That's all. Didn't talk to me, Mr 'Baas' Bradley, Line

Supervisor, or anybody. He didn't even look at the plant!
And what did I see when those three Galaxies disappeared?
The white staff at the main switchboard.
'Double speed on the line! Make up for production lost!'
It ended up with us working harder that bloody day than
ever before. Just because that big. . . . [*shakes his head.*]
Six years there. Six years a bloody fool.

[*Back to his newspaper. A few more headlines with appropriate
comment, then. . . .*]

[*Reading*] 'The Mass Murderer! Doom!'

[*Smile of recognition.*]

'For fleas . . . Doom. Flies . . . Doom. Bedbugs . . . Doom. For
cockroaches and other household pests. The household in-
secticide . . . Doom.' Useful stuff. Remember, Styles? *Ja*.
[*To the audience.*] After all that time at Ford I sat down one
day. I said to myself:
'Styles, you're a bloody monkey, boy!'
'What do you mean?'
'You're a monkey, man.'
'Go to hell!'
'Come on, Styles, you're a monkey, man, and you know it. Run
up and down the whole bloody day! Your life doesn't belong
to you. You've sold it. For what, Styles? Gold wrist-watch
in twenty-five years time when they sign you off because
you're too old for anything any more?'
I was right. I took a good look at my life. What did I see?
A bloody circus monkey! Selling most of his time on this earth
to another man. Out of every twenty-four hours I could only
properly call mine the six when I was sleeping. What the hell
is the use of that?
Think about it, friend. Wake up in the morning, half-past
six, out of the pyjamas and into the bath-tub, put on your
shirt with one hand, socks with the other, realize you got your
shoes on the wrong bloody feet, and all the time the seconds
are passing and if you don't hurry up you'll miss the bus. . . .
'Get the lunch, dear. I'm late. My lunch, please, darling! . . .
then the children come in . . . 'Daddy, can I have this?
Daddy, I want money for that.' 'Go to your mother. I
haven't got time. Look after the children, please, sweetheart!!'

... grab your lunch ... 'Bye Bye!!' and then run like I-don't-know-what for the bus stop. You call that living? I went back to myself for another chat:

'Suppose you're right. What then?'

'Try something else.'

'Like what?'

Silly question to ask. I knew what I was going to say. Photographer! It was my hobby in those days. I used to pick up a few cents on the side taking cards at parties, weddings, big occasions. But when it came to telling my wife and parents that I wanted to turn professional ... !!

My father was the worst.

'You call that work? Click-click with a camera. Are you mad?'

I tried to explain. 'Daddy, if I could stand on my own two feet and not be somebody else's tool, I'd have some respect for myself. I'd be a man.'

'What do you mean? Aren't you one already? You're circumcised, you've got a wife. ...'

Talk about the generation gap!

Anyway I thought: To hell with them. I'm trying it.

It was the Christmas shutdown, so I had lots of time to look around for a studio. My friend Dhlamini at the Funeral Parlour told me about a vacant room next door. He encouraged me. I remember his words. 'Grab your chance, Styles. Grab it before somebody in my line puts you in a box and closes the lid.' I applied for permission to use the room as a studio. After some time the first letter back:

'Your application has been received and is being considered.' A month later: 'The matter is receiving the serious consideration of the Board.' Another month: 'Your application is now on the director's table.' I nearly gave up, friends. But one day, a knock at the door—the postman—I had to sign for a registered letter. 'We are pleased to inform you. ...'

[*Styles has a good laugh.*]

I ran all the way to the Administration Offices, grabbed the key, ran all the way back to Red Location, unlocked the door, and walked in!

What I found sobered me up a little bit. Window panes were all broken; big hole in the roof, cobwebs in the corners. I didn't let that put me off though. Said to myself: 'This is your chance, Styles. Grab it.' Some kids helped me clean it out. The dust! *Yo!* When the broom walked in the Sahara Desert walked out! But at the end of that day it was reasonably clean. I stood here in the middle of the floor, straight! You know what that means? To stand straight in a place of your own? To be your own . . . General Foreman, Mr 'Baas', Line Supervisor—the lot! I was tall, six foot six and doing my own inspection of the plant.

So I'm standing there—here—feeling big and what do I see on the walls? Cockroaches. *Ja*, cockroaches . . . in *my* place. I don't mean those little things that run all over the place when you pull out the kitchen drawer. I'm talking about the big bastards, the paratroopers as we call them. I didn't like them. I'm not afraid of them but I just don't like them! All over. On the floors, the walls. I heard the one on the wall say: 'What's going on? Who opened the door?' The one on the floor answered: 'Relax. He won't last. This place is condemned.' That's when I thought: Doom.

Out of here and into the Chinaman's shop. 'Good day, sir. I've got a problem. Cockroaches.'

The Chinaman didn't even think, man, he just said: 'Doom!' I said: 'Certainly.' He said: 'Doom, seventy-five cents a tin.' Paid him for two and went back. *Yo!* You should have seen me! Two-tin Charlie!

[*His two tins at the ready, forefingers on the press-buttons, Styles gives us a graphic re-enactment of what happened. There is a brief respite to 'reload'—shake the tins—and tie a handkerchief around his nose after which he returns to the fight. Styles eventually backs through the imaginary door, still firing, and closes it. Spins the tins and puts them into their holsters.*]

I went home to sleep. *I* went to sleep. Not them [*the cockroaches*]. What do you think happened here? General meeting under the floorboards. All the bloody survivors. The old professor addressed them: 'Brothers, we face a problem of serious pollution . . . contamination! The menace appears to be called Doom. I have recommended a general inoculation of the whole community. Everybody in line, please. [*Inoculation proceeds.*] Next . . . next . . . next. . . .' While poor old Styles is

smiling in his sleep! Next morning I walked in. . . . [*He stops abruptly.*] . . . What's this? Cockroach walking on the floor? Another one on the ceiling? Not a damn! Doom did it yesterday. Doom does it today. [*Whips out the two tins and goes in fighting. This time, however, it is not long before they peter out.*] Pssssssss . . . pssssss . . . pssss . . . pss [*a last desperate shake, but he barely manages to get out a squirt*].
Pss.
No bloody good! The old bastard on the floor just waved his feelers in the air as if he was enjoying air-conditioning.
I went next door to Dhlamini and told him about my problem. He laughed. 'Doom? You're wasting your time, Styles. You want to solve your problem, get a cat. What do you think a cat lives on in the township? Milk? If there's any the baby gets it. Meat? When the family sees it only once a week? Mice? The little boys got rid of them years ago. Insects, man, township cats are insect-eaters. Here. . . .'
He gave me a little cat. I'm . . . I'm not too fond of cats normally. This one was called Blackie . . . I wasn't too fond of that name either. But . . . Kitsy! Kitsy! Kitsy . . . little Blackie followed me back to the studio.
The next morning when I walked in what do you think I saw? Wings. I smiled. Because one thing I do know is that no cockroach can take his wings off. He's dead!

[*Proud gesture taking in the whole of his studio.*]
So here it is!

[*To his name-board.*]

'Styles Photographic Studio. Reference Books; Passports; Weddings; Engagements; Birthday Parties and Parties. Proprietor: Styles.'
When you look at this, what do you see? Just another photographic studio? Where people come because they've lost their Reference Book and need a photo for the new one? That I sit them down, set up the camera . . . 'No expression, please.' . . . click-click . . . 'Come back tomorrow, please' . . . and then kick them out and wait for the next? No, friend. It's more than just that. This is a strong-room of dreams. The dreamers? My people. The simple people, who you never find mentioned in the history books, who never get statues

erected to them, or monuments commemorating their great deeds. People who would be forgotten, and their dreams with them, if it wasn't for Styles. That's what I do, friends. Put down, in my way, on paper the dreams and hopes of my people so that even their children's children will remember a man . . . 'This was our Grandfather' . . . and say his name. Walk into the houses of New Brighton and on the walls you'll find hanging the story of the people the writers of the big books forget about.

[*To his display-board.*]

This one [*a photograph*] walked in here one morning. I was just passing the time. Midweek. Business is always slow then. Anyway, a knock at the door. Yes! I must explain something. I get two types of knock here. When I hear . . . [*knocks solemnly on the table*] . . . I don't even look up, man. 'Funeral parlour is next door.' But when I hear . . . [*energetic rap on the table . . . he laughs*] . . . that's *my* sound, and I shout 'Come in!'

In walked a chap, full of smiles, little parcel under his arm. I can still see him, man!

[*Styles acts both roles.*]

'Mr Styles?'
I said: 'Come in!'
'Mr Styles, I've come to take a snap, Mr Styles.'
I said: 'Sit down! Sit down, my friend!'
'No, Mr Styles. I want to take the snap standing. [*Barely containing his suppressed excitement and happiness*] Mr Styles, take the card, please!'
I said: 'Certainly, friend.'
Something you mustn't do is interfere with a man's dream. If he wants to do it standing, let him stand. If he wants to sit, let him sit. Do exactly what they want! Sometimes they come in here, all smart in a suit, then off comes the jacket and shoes and socks . . . [*adopts a boxer's stance*] . . . 'Take it, Mr Styles. Take it!' And I take it. No questions! Start asking stupid questions and you destroy that dream. Anyway, this chap I'm telling you about . . . [*laughing warmly as he remembers*] . . . I've seen a lot of smiles in my business, friends, but that one gets first prize. I set up my camera, and just as I was ready

to go . . . 'Wait, wait, Mr Styles! I want you to take the card with this.' Out of his parcel came a long piece of white paper . . . looked like some sort of document . . . he held it in front of him. [*Styles demonstrates.*] For once I didn't have to say, 'Smile!' Just: 'Hold it!' . . . and, click, . . . finished. I asked him what the document was.

'You see, Mr Styles, I'm forty-eight years old. I work twenty-two years for the municipality and the foreman kept on saying to me if I want promotion to Boss-boy I must try to better my education. I didn't write well, Mr Styles. So I took a course with the Damelin Correspondence College. Seven years, Mr Styles! And at last I made it. Here it is. Standard Six Certificate, School Leaving, Third Class! I made it, Mr Styles. I made it. But I'm not finished. I'm going to take up for the Junior Certificate, then Matric . . . and you watch, Mr Styles. One day I walk out of my house, graduate, self-made! Bye-bye, Mr Styles,' . . . and he walked out of here happy man, self-made.

[*Back to his display-board; another photograph.*]

My best. Family Card. You know the Family Card? Good for business. Lot of people and they all want copies.

One Saturday morning. Suddenly a hell of a noise outside in the street. I thought: What's going on now? Next thing that door burst open and in they came! First the little ones, then the five- and six-year-olds. . . . I didn't know what was going on, man! Stupid children, coming to mess up my place. I was still trying to chse them out when the bigger boys and girls came through the door. Then it clicked. Family Card!

[*Changing his manner abruptly.*]

'Come in! Come in!'

[*Ushering a crowd of people into his studio.*]

. . . now the young men and women were coming in, then the mothers and fathers, uncles and aunties . . . the eldest son, a mature man, and finally . . .

[*Shaking his head with admiration at the memory.*]

the Old Man, the Grandfather! [*The 'old man' walks slowly and with dignity into the studio and sits down in the chair.*]

I looked at him. His grey hair was a sign of wisdom. His face, weather-beaten and lined with experience. Looking at it was like paging the volume of his history, written by himself. He was a living symbol of Life, of all it means and does to a man. I adored him. He sat there—half smiling, half serious—as if he had already seen the end of his road.

The eldest son said to me: 'Mr Styles, this is my father, my mother, my brothers and sisters, their wives and husbands, our children. Twenty-seven of us, Mr Styles. We have come to take a card. My father . . . ,' he pointed to the old man, '. . . my father always wanted it.'

I said: 'Certainly. Leave the rest to me.' I went to work.

[*Another graphic re-enactment of the scene as he describes it.*]

The old lady here, the eldest son there. Then the other one, with the other one. On this side I did something with the daughters, aunties, and one bachelor brother. Then in front of it all the eight-to-twelves, standing, in front of them the four-to-sevens, kneeling, and finally right on the floor everything that was left, sitting. Jesus, it was hard work, but finally I had them all sorted out and I went behind the camera.

[*Behind his camera.*]

Just starting to focus . . .

[*Imaginary child in front of the lens; Styles chases the child back to the family group.*]

'. . . Sit down! Sit down!'

Back to the camera, start to focus again. . . . Not One Of Them Was Smiling! I tried the old trick. 'Say cheese, please.' At first they just looked at me. 'Come on! Cheese!' The children were the first to pick it up.

[*Child's voice.*] 'Cheese. Cheese. Cheese.' Then the ones a little bit bigger—'Cheese'—then the next lot—'Cheese'—the uncles and aunties—'Cheese'—and finally the old man himself—'Cheese'! I thought the roof was going off, man! People outside in the street came and looked through the window. They joined in: 'Cheese.' When I looked again the mourners from the funeral parlour were there wiping away their tears and saying 'Cheese'. Pressed my little button and there it was—New Brighton's smile, twenty-seven variations. Don't you believe those bloody fools who make out we don't know how to smile!

Anyway, you should have seen me then. Moved the bachelor this side, sister-in-laws that side. Put the eldest son behind the old man. Reorganized the children. . . . [*Back behind his camera.*] 'Once again, please! Cheese!' Back to work . . . old man and old woman together, daughters behind them, sons on the side. Those that were kneeling now standing, those that were standing, now kneeling. . . . Ten times, friends! Each one different!

[*An exhausted Styles collapses in a chair.*]

When they walked out finally I almost said Never Again! A week later the eldest son came back for the cards. I had them ready. The moment he walked through that door I could see he was in trouble. He said to me: 'Mr Styles, we almost didn't make it. My father died two days after the card. He will never see it.' 'Come on,' I said. 'You're a man. One day or the other everyone of us must go home. Here. . . .' I grabbed the cards. 'Here. Look at your father and thank God for the time he was given on this earth.' We went through them together. He looked at them in silence. After the third one, the tear went slowly down his cheek.

But at the same time . . . I was watching him carefully . . . something started to happen as he saw his father there with himself, his brothers and sisters, and all the little grandchildren. He began to smile. 'That's it, brother,' I said. 'Smile! Smile at your father. Smile at the world.'

When he left, I thought of him going back to his little house somewhere in New Brighton, filled that day with the little mothers in black because a man had died. I saw my cards passing from hand to hand. I saw hands wipe away tears, and then the first timid little smiles.

You must understand one thing. We own nothing except ourselves. This world and its laws, allows us nothing, except ourselves. There is nothing we can leave behind when we die, except the memory of ourselves. I know what I'm talking about, friends—I had a father, and he died.

[*To the display-board.*]

Here he is. My father. That's him. Fought in the war. Second

World War. Fought at Tobruk. In Egypt. He fought in France so that this country and all the others could stay Free. When he came back they stripped him at the docks—his gun, his uniform, the dignity they'd allowed him for a few mad years because the world needed men to fight and be ready to sacrifice themselves for something called Freedom. In return they let him keep his scoff-tin and gave him a bicycle. Size twenty-eight. I remember, because it was too big for me. When he died, in a rotten old suitcase amongst some of his old rags, I found that photograph. That's all. That's all I have from him.

[*The display-board again.*]

Or this old lady. Mrs Matothlana. Used to stay in Sangocha Street. You remember! Her husband was arrested. . . .

[*Knock at the door.*]

Tell you about it later. Come in!

[A man *walks nervously into the studio. Dressed in an ill-fitting new double-breasted suit. He is carrying a plastic bag with a hat in it. His manner is hesitant and shy. Styles takes one look at him and breaks into an enormous smile.*]

[*An aside to the audience*] A Dream!

[*To the man.*] Come in, my friend.

MAN. Mr Styles?

STYLES. That's me. Come in! You have come to take a card?

MAN. Snap.

STYLES. Yes, a card. Have you got a deposit?

MAN. Yes.

STYLES. Good. Let me just take your name down. You see, you pay deposit now, and when you come for the card, you pay the rest.

MAN. Yes.

STYLES [*to his desk and a black book for names and addresses*]. What is your name? [*The man hesitates, as if not sure of himself.*] Your name, please?

[*Pause.*]

Come on, my friend. You must surely have a name.

MAN [*pulling himself together, but still very nervous*]. Robert Zwelinzima.

STYLES [*writing*]. 'Robert Zwelinzima.' Address?

MAN [*swallowing*]. Fifty, Mapija Street.

STYLES [*writes, then pauses*]. 'Fifty, Mapija?'

MAN. Yes.

STYLES. You staying with Buntu?

MAN. Buntu.

STYLES. Very good somebody that one. Came here for his Wedding Card. Always helping people. If that man was white they'd call him a liberal.

[*Now finished writing. Back to his customer.*]

All right. How many cards do you want?

MAN. One card.

STYLES [*disappointed*]. Only one?

MAN. One.

STYLES. How do you want to take the card?

[*The man is not sure of what the question means.*]

You can take the card standing . . .

[*Styles strikes a stylish pose next to the table.*]

sitting . . .

[*Another pose . . . this time in the chair.*]

anyhow. How do you want it?

MAN. Anyhow.

STYLES. Right. Sit down.

[*Robert hesitates.*]

Sit down!

[*Styles fetches a vase with plastic flowers, dusts them off, and places them on the table. Robert holds up his plastic bag.*]

What you got there?

[*Out comes the hat.*]

Aha! Stetson. Put it on, my friend.

[*Robert handles it shyly.*]

You can put it on, Robert.

[*Robert pulls it on. Styles does up one of his jacket buttons.*]

18

What a beautiful suit, my friend! Where did you buy it?

MAN. Sales House.

STYLES [*quoting a sales slogan*]. 'Where the Black world buys the best. Six months to pay. Pay as you wear.'

[*Nudges Robert.*]

. . . and they never repossess!

[*They share a laugh.*]

What are you going to do with this card?

[*Chatting away as he goes to his camera and sets it up for the photo. Robert watches the preparations apprehensively.*]

MAN. Send it to my wife.

STYLES. Your wife!

MAN. Nowetu.

STYLES. Where's your wife?

MAN. King William's Town.

STYLES [*exaggerated admiration*]. At last! The kind of man I like. Not one of those foolish young boys who come here to find work and then forget their families back home. A man, with responsibility!

Where do you work?

MAN. Feltex.

STYLES. I hear they pay good there.

MAN. Not bad.

[*He is now very tense, staring fixedly at the camera. Styles straightens up behind it.*]

STYLES. Come on, Robert! You want your wife to get a card with her husband looking like he's got all the worries in the world on his back? What will she think? 'My poor husband is in trouble!' You must smile!

[*Robert shamefacedly relaxes a little and starts to smile.*]

That's it!

[*He relaxes still more. Beginning to enjoy himself. Uncertainly produces a very fancy pipe from one of his pockets.*
Styles now really warming to the assignment.]

Look, have you ever walked down the passage to the office with the big glass door and the board outside: 'Manager—

Bestuurder'. Imagine it, man, you, Robert Zwelinzima, behind a desk in an office like that! It can happen, Robert. Quick promotion to Chief Messenger. I'll show you what we do.

[*Styles produces a Philips' class-room map of the world, which he hangs behind the table as a backdrop to the photo.*]

Look at it, Robert. America, England, Africa, Russia, Asia!

[*Carried away still further by his excitement, Styles finds a cigarette, lights it, and gives it to Robert to hold. The latter is now ready for the 'card' . . . pipe in one hand and cigarette in the other. Styles stands behind his camera and admires his handiwork.*]

Mr Robert Zwelinzima, Chief Messenger at Feltex, sitting in his office with the world behind him. Smile, Robert. Smile!

[*Studying his subject through the viewfinder of the camera.*]

Lower your hand, Robert . . . towards the ashtray . . . more . . . now make a four with your legs. . . .

[*He demonstrates behind the camera. Robert crosses his legs.*]

Hold it, Robert. . . . Keep on smiling . . . that's it. . . . [*presses the release button—the shutter clicks.*]

Beautiful! All right, Robert.

[*Robert and his smile remain frozen.*]

Robert. You can relax now. It's finished!

MAN. Finished?

STYLES. Yes. You just want the one card?

MAN. Yes.

STYLES. What happens if you lose it? Hey? I've heard stories about those postmen, Robert. *Yo!* Sit on the side of the road and open the letters they should be delivering! 'Dear wife . . .' —one rand this side, letter thrown away. 'Dear wife . . .'— another rand this side, letter thrown away. You want that to happen to you? Come on! What about a movie, man?

MAN. Movie?

STYLES. Don't you know the movie?

MAN. No.

STYLES. Simple! You just walk you see . . .

[*Styles demonstrates; at a certain point freezes in mid-stride.*]

. . . and I take the card! Then you can write to your wife:

'Dear wife, I am coming home at Christmas. . . .' Put the card in your letter and post it. Your wife opens the letter and what does she see? Her Robert, walking home to her! She shows it to the children. 'Look, children, your daddy is coming!' The children jump and clap their hands: 'Daddy is coming! Daddy is coming!'

MAN [*excited by the picture Styles has conjured up*]. All right!

STYLES. You want a movie?

MAN. I want a movie.

STYLES. That's my man! Look at this, Robert.

[*Styles reverses the map hanging behind the table to reveal a gaudy painting of a futuristic city.*]

City of the Future! Look at it. Mr Robert Zwelinzima, man about town, future head of Feltex, walking through the City of the Future!

MAN [*examining the backdrop with admiration. He recognizes a landmark*]. OK.

STYLES. OK Bazaars . . . [*the other buildings*] . . . Mutual Building Society, Barclays Bank . . . the lot!
What you looking for, Robert?

MAN. Feltex.

STYLES. Yes . . . well, you see, I couldn't fit everything on, Robert. But if I had had enough space Feltex would have been here.

[*To his table for props.*]

Walking-stick . . . newspaper. . . .

MAN [*diffidently*]. I don't read.

STYLES. That is not important, my friend. You think all those monkeys carrying newspapers can read? They look at the pictures.

[*After 'dressing' Robert with the props he moves back to his camera.*]

This is going to be beautiful, Robert. My best card. I must send one to the magazines.

All right, Robert, now move back. Remember what I showed you. Just walk towards me and right in front of the City of the Future. I'll take the picture. Ready? Now come, Robert. . . .

[*Pipe in mouth, walking-stick in hand, newspaper under the other*

*arm, Robert takes a jaunty step and then freezes, as Styles had
shown him earlier.*]

Come, Robert. . . .

[*Another step.*]

Just one more, Robert. . . .

[*Another step.*]

Stop! Hold it, Robert. Hold it!

[*The camera flash goes off; simultaneously a blackout except for
one light on Robert, frozen in the pose that will appear in the
picture. We are in fact looking at the photograph. It 'comes to
life' and dictates the letter that will accompany it to Nowetu in
King William's Town.*]

MAN. Nowetu . . .

[*Correcting himself.*]

Dear Nowetu,

I've got wonderful news for you in this letter. My troubles
are over, I think. You won't believe it, but I must tell you.
Sizwe Bansi, in a manner of speaking, is dead! I'll tell you
what I can.

As you know, when I left the Railway Compound I went to
stay with a friend of mine called Zola. A very good friend
that, Nowetu. In fact he was even trying to help me find some
job. But that's not easy, Nowetu, because Port Elizabeth is a
big place, a very big place with lots of factories but also
lots of people looking for a job like me. There are so many
men, Nowetu, who have left their places because they are dry
and have come here to find work!

After a week with Zola, I was in big trouble. The headman
came around, and after a lot of happenings which I will tell
you when I see you, they put a stamp in my passbook
which said I must leave Port Elizabeth at once in three
days time. I was very much unhappy, Nowetu. I couldn't
stay with Zola because if the headman found me there again
my troubles would be even bigger. So Zola took me to a friend
of his called Buntu, and asked him if I could stay with him
until I decided what to do. . . .

[*Buntu's house in New Brighton. Table and two chairs. Robert, in
a direct continuation of the preceding scene, is already there, as Buntu,*

jacket slung over his shoulder, walks in. Holds out his hand to Robert.]

BUNTU. Hi. Buntu.

[*They shake hands.*]

MAN. Sizwe Bansi.

BUNTU. Sit down.

[*They sit.*]

Zola told me you were coming. Didn't have time to explain anything. Just asked if you could spend a few nights here. You can perch yourself on that sofa in the corner. I'm alone at the moment. My wife is a domestic . . . sleep-in at Kabega Park . . . only comes home weekends. Hot today, hey?

[*In the course of this scene Buntu will busy himself first by having a wash—basin and jug of water on the table—and then by changing from his working clothes preparatory to going out. Sizwe Bansi stays in his chair.*]

What's your problem, friend?

MAN. I've got no permit to stay in Port Elizabeth.

BUNTU. Where do you have a permit to stay?

MAN. King William's Town.

BUNTU. How did they find out?

MAN [*tells his story with the hesitation and uncertainty of the illiterate. When words fail him he tries to use his hands.*]
I was staying with Zola, as you know. I was very happy there. But one night . . . I was sleeping on the floor . . . I heard some noises and when I looked up I saw torches shining in through the window . . . then there was a loud knocking on the door. When I got up Zola was there in the dark . . . he was trying to whisper something. I think he was saying I must hide. So I crawled under the table. The headman came in and looked around and found me hiding under the table . . . and dragged me out.

BUNTU. Raid?

MAN. Yes, it was a raid. I was just wearing my pants. My shirt was lying on the other side. I just managed to grab it as they were pushing me out. . . . I finished dressing in the van. They drove straight to the administration office . . . and then from there they drove to the Labour Bureau. I was made to stand in the passage there, with everybody looking at me and shaking their heads like they knew I was in big trouble. Later I was taken into an office and made to stand next to the door.... The white man behind the desk had my book and he also looked at me and shook his head. Just then one other white man came in with a card. . . .

BUNTU. A card?

MAN. He was carrying a card.

BUNTU. Pink card?

MAN. Yes, the card was pink.

BUNTU. Record card. Your whole bloody life is written down on that. Go on.

MAN. Then the first white man started writing something on the card . . . and just then somebody came in carrying a. . . .

[*demonstrates what he means by banging a clenched fist on the table.*]

BUNTU. A stamp?

MAN. Yes, a stamp. [*Repeats the action.*] He was carrying a stamp.

BUNTU. And then?

MAN. He put it on my passbook.

BUNTU. Let me see your book?

[*Sizwe produces his passbook from the back-pocket of his trousers. Buntu examines it.*]

Shit! You know what this is? [*The stamp.*]

MAN. I can't read.

BUNTU. Listen . . . [*reads*]. 'You are required to report to the Bantu Affairs Commissioner, King William's Town, within three days of the above-mentioned date for the. . . .' You should have been home yesterday! . . . 'for the purpose of repatriation to home district.' Influx Control.
You're in trouble, Sizwe.

MAN. I don't want to leave Port Elizabeth.

BUNTU. Maybe. But if that book says go, you go.

MAN. Can't I maybe burn this book and get a new one?

BANTU. Burn that book? Stop kidding yourself, Sizwe! Anyway

suppose you do. You must immediately go apply for a new one. Right? And until that new one comes, be careful the police don't stop you and ask for your book. Into the Court-room, brother. Charge: Failing to produce Reference Book on Demand. Five rand or five days. Finally the new book comes. Down to the Labour Bureau for a stamp . . . it's got to be endorsed with permission to be in this area. White man at the Labour Bureau takes the book, looks at it—doesn't look at you!—goes to the big machine and feeds in your number . . .

[*Buntu goes through the motions of punching out a number on a computer.*]

. . . card jumps out, he reads: 'Sizwe Bansi. Endorsed to King William's Town. . . .' Takes your book, fetches that same stamp, and in it goes again. So you burn that book, or throw it away, and get another one. Same thing happens.

[*Buntu feeds the computer; the card jumps out.*]

'Sizwe Bansi. Endorsed to King William's Town. . . .' Stamp goes in the third time. . . . But this time it's also into a van and off to the Native Commissioner's Office; card around your neck with your number on it; escort on both sides and back to King William's Town. They make you pay for the train fare too!

MAN. I think I will try to look for some jobs in the garden.

BUNTU. You? Job as a garden-boy? Don't you read the newspapers?

MAN. I can't read.

BUNTU. I'll tell you what the little white ladies say: 'Domestic vacancies. I want a garden-boy with good manners and a wide knowledge of seasons and flowers. Book in order.' Yours in order? Anyway what the hell do you know about seasons and flowers? [*After a moment's thought.*] Do you know any white man who's prepared to give you a job?

MAN. No. I don't know any white man.

BUNTU. Pity. We might have been able to work something then. You talk to the white man, you see, and ask him to write a letter saying he's got a job for you. You take that letter from the white man and go back to King William's Town, where you show it to the Native Commissioner there. The Native Commissioner in King William's Town reads that letter

25

from the white man in Port Elizabeth who is ready to give you the job. He then writes a letter back to the Native Commissioner in Port Elizabeth. So you come back here with the two letters. Then the Native Commissioner in Port Elizabeth reads the letter from the Native Commissioner in King William's Town together with the first letter from the white man who is prepared to give you a job, and he says when he reads the letters: Ah yes, this man Sizwe Bansi can get a job. So the Native Commissioner in Port Elizabeth then writes a letter which you take with the letters from the Native Commissioner in King William's Town and the white man in Port Elizabeth, to the Senior Officer at the Labour Bureau, who reads all the letters. Then he will put the right stamp in your book and give you another letter from himself which together with the letters from the white man and the two Native Affairs Commissioners, you take to the Administration Office here in New Brighton and make an application for Residence Permit, so that you don't fall victim of raids again. Simple.

MAN. Maybe I can start a little business selling potatoes and. . . .

BUNTU. Where do you get the potatoes and . . .?

MAN. I'll buy them.

BUNTU. With what?

MAN. Borrow some money. . . .

BUNTU. Who is going to lend money to a somebody endorsed to hell and gone out in the bush? And how you going to buy your potatoes at the market without a Hawker's Licence? Same story, Sizwe. You won't get that because of the bloody stamp in your book.

There's no way out, Sizwe. You're not the first one who has tried to find it. Take my advice and catch that train back to King William's Town. If you need work so bad go knock on the door of the Mines Recruiting Office. Dig gold for the white man. That's the only time they don't worry about Influx Control.

MAN. I don't want to work on the mines. There is no money there. And it's dangerous, under the ground. Many black men get killed when the rocks fall. You can die there.

BUNTU [*stopped by the last remark into taking possibly his first real look at Sizwe*].

You don't want to die.

MAN. I don't want to die.

BUNTU [*stops whatever he is doing to sit down and talk to Sizwe with an intimacy that was not there before.*]

You married, Sizwe?

MAN. Yes.

BUNTU. How many children?

MAN. I've got four children.

BUNTU. Boys? Girls?

MAN. I've got three boys and one girl.

BUNTU. Schooling?

MAN. Two are schooling. The other two stay at home with their mother.

BUNTU. Your wife is not working.

MAN. The place where we stay is fifteen miles from town. There is only one shop there. Baas van Wyk. He has already got a woman working for him. King William's Town is a dry place Mr Buntu . . . very small and too many people. That is why I don't want to go back.

BUNTU. *Ag*, friend I don't know! I'm also married. One child.

MAN. Only one?

BUNTU. *Ja*, my wife attends this Birth Control Clinic rubbish. The child is staying with my mother.

[*Shaking his head.*] *Hai*, Sizwe! If I had to tell you the trouble I had before I could get the right stamps in my book, even though I was born in this area! The trouble I had before I could get a decent job . . . born in this area! The trouble I had to get this two-roomed house . . . born in this area!

MAN. Why is there so much trouble, Mr Buntu?

BUNTU. Two weeks back I went to a funeral with a friend of mine. Out in the country. An old relative of his passed away. Usual thing . . . sermons in the house, sermons in the church, sermons at the graveside. I thought they were never going to stop talking!

At the graveside service there was one fellow, a lay preacher . . . short man, neat little moustache, wearing one of those old-fashioned double-breasted black suits. . . . *Haai!* He was wonderful. While he talked he had a gesture with his hands . . . like this . . . that reminded me of our youth, when we learnt to fight with kieries. His text was 'Going Home'. He handled it well, Sizwe. Started by saying that the first man to sign the Death Contract with God, was Adam, when he sinned in Eden. Since that day, wherever Man is, or whatever he does, he is never without his faithful companion, Death. So with Outa Jacob . . . the dead man's name . . . he has at last accepted the terms of his contract with God.

But in his life, friends, he walked the roads of this land. He helped print those footpaths which lead through the bush and over the veld . . . footpaths which his children are now walking. He worked on farms from this district down to the coast and north as far as Pretoria. I knew him. He was a friend. Many people knew Outa Jacob. For a long time he worked for Baas van der Walt. But when the old man died his young son Hendrik said: 'I don't like you. Go!' Outa Jacob picked up his load and put it on his shoulders. His wife followed. He went to the next farm . . . through the fence, up to the house . . . : 'Work, please, Baas.' Baas Potgieter took him. He stayed a long time there too, until one day there was trouble between the Madam and his wife. Jacob and his wife were walking again. The load on his back was heavier, he wasn't so young any more, and there were children behind them now as well. On to the next farm. No work. The next one. No work. Then the next one. A little time there. But the drought was bad and the farmer said: 'Sorry, Jacob. The cattle are dying. I'm moving to the city.' Jacob picked up his load yet again. So it went, friends. On and on . . . until he arrived there. [*The grave at his feet.*] Now at last it's over. No matter how hard-arsed the boer on this farm wants to be, he cannot move Outa Jacob. He has reached Home.

[*Pause.*]

That's it, brother. The only time we'll find peace is when they dig a hole for us and press our face into the earth.

[*Putting on his coat.*]

Ag, to hell with it. If we go on like this much longer we'll do the digging for them.

[*Changing his tone.*]

You know Sky's place, Sizwe?

MAN. No.

BUNTU. Come. Let me give you a treat. I'll do you there.

[*Exit Buntu.*
*Blackout except for a light on Sizwe. He continues his letter
to Nowetu.*]

MAN. Sky's place? [*Shakes his head and laughs.*] Hey, Nowetu!
When I mention that name again, I get a headache ... the
same headache I had when I woke up in Buntu's place the
next morning. You won't believe what it was like. You cannot!
It would be like you walking down Pickering Street in
King William's Town and going into Koekemoer's Café to
buy bread, and what do you see sitting there at the smart table
and chairs? Your husband, Sizwe Bansi, being served ice-
cream and cool drinks by old Mrs Koekemoer herself. Such
would be your surprise if you had seen me at Sky's place.
Only they weren't serving cool drinks and ice-cream. No!
First-class booze, Nowetu. And it wasn't old Mrs Koekemoer
serving me, but a certain lovely and beautiful lady called
Miss Nkonyemi. And it wasn't just your husband Sizwe sitting
there with all the most important people of New Brighton, but
Mister Bansi.

[*He starts to laugh.*]

Mister Bansi!

[*As the laugh gets bigger, Sizwe rises to his feet.*]

[*The street outside Sky's Shebeen in New Brighton. Our man is
amiably drunk. He addresses the audience.*]

MAN. Do you know who I am, friend? Take my hand, friend.
Take my hand. I am Mister Bansi, friend. Do you know where
I come from? I come from Sky's place, friend. A most wonderful place. I met everybody there, good people. I've been
drinking, my friends—brandy, wine, beer. ... Don't you want
to go in there, good people? Let's all go to Sky's place.
[*Shouting.*] Mr Buntu! Mr Buntu!

[*Buntu enters shouting goodbye to friends at the Shebeen. He joins
Sizwe. Buntu, though not drunk, is also amiably talkative under
the influence of a good few drinks.*]

BUNTU [*discovering the audience*]. Hey, where did you get all these wonderful people?

MAN. I just found them here, Mr Buntu.

BUNTU. Wonderful!

MAN. I'm inviting them to Sky's place, Mr Buntu.

BUNTU. You tell them about Sky's?

MAN. I told them about Sky's place, Mr Buntu.

BUNTU [*to the audience*]. We been having a time there, man!

MAN. They know it. I told them everything.

BUNTU [*laughing*]. Sizwe! We had our fun there.

MAN. Hey . . . hey. . . .

BUNTU. Remember that Member of the Advisory Board?

MAN. Hey. . . . Hey . . . Mr Buntu! You know I respect you, friend. You must call me nice.

BUNTU. What do you mean?

MAN [*clumsy dignity*]. I'm not just Sizwe no more. He might have walked in, but Mr Bansi walked out!

BUNTU [*playing along*]. I am terribly sorry, Mr Bansi. I apologize for my familiarity. Please don't be offended.

[*Handing over one of the two oranges he is carrying.*]

Allow me . . . with the compliments of Miss Nkonyeni.

MAN [*taking the orange with a broad but sheepish grin*]. Miss Nkonyeni!

BUNTU. Sweet dreams, Mr Bansi.

MAN [*tears the orange with his thumbs and starts eating it messily*]. Lovely lady, Mr Buntu.

BUNTU [*leaves Sizwe with a laugh. To the audience*]. Back there in the Shebeen a Member of the Advisory Board hears that he comes from King William's Town. He goes up to Sizwe. 'Tell me, Mr Bansi, what do you think of Ciskeian Independence?'

MAN [*interrupting*]. *Ja*, I remember that one. Bloody Mister Member of the Advisory Board. Talking about Ciskeian Independence!

[*To the audience.*]

I must tell you, friend . . . when a car passes or the wind blows

up the dust, Ciskeian Independence makes you cough. I'm
telling you, friend . . . put a man in a pondok and call that
Independence? My good friend, let me tell you . . . Ciskeian
Independence is shit!

BUNTU Or that other chap! Old Jolobe. The fat tycoon man!
[to the audience] Comes to me . . . [pompous voice] . . . 'Your friend,
Mr Bansi, is he on an official visit to town?' 'No,' I said,
'Mr Bansi is on an official walkout!' [Buntu thinks this is a big
joke.]

MAN [stubbornly]. I'm here to stay.

BUNTU [looking at his watch]. Hey, Sizwe. . . .

MAN [reproachfully]. Mr Buntu!

BUNTU [correcting himself]. Mr Bansi, it is getting late. I've
got to work tomorrow. Care to lead the way, Mr Bansi?

MAN. You think I can't? You think Mr Bansi is lost?

BUNTU. I didn't say that.

MAN. You are thinking it, friend. I'll show you. This is Chinga
Street.

BUNTU. Very good! But which way do we . . . ?

MAN [setting off]. This way.

BUNTU [pulling him back]. Mistake. You're heading for Site
and Service and a lot of trouble with the Tsotsis.

MAN [the opposite direction]. That way.

BUNTU. Lead on. I'm right behind you.

MAN. Ja, you are right, Mr Buntu. There is Newell High
School. Now. . . .

BUNTU. Think carefully!

MAN. . . . when we were going to Sky's we had Newell in front.
So when we leave Sky's we put Newell behind.

BUNTU. Very good!

[An appropriate change in direction. They continue walking, and
eventually arrive at a square, with roads leading off in many directions.
Sizwe is lost. He wanders around, uncertain of the direction to
take.]

MAN. Haai, Mr Buntu . . . !

BUNTU. Mbizweni Square.

MAN. *Yo!* Cross-roads to hell, wait . . . [*Closer look at landmark.*] . . . that building . . . Rio Cinema! So we must. . . .

BUNTU. Rio Cinema? With a white cross on top, bell outside, and the big show on Sundays?

MAN [*sheepishly*]. You're right, friend. I've got it, Mr Buntu. That way.

[*He starts off. Buntu watches him.*]

BUNTU. Goodbye. King William's Town a hundred and fifty miles. Don't forget to write.

MAN [*hurried about-turn*]. *Haai . . . haai. . . .*

BUNTU. Okay, Sizwe, I'll take over from here. But just hang on for a second I want to have a piss. Don't move!

[*Buntu disappears into the dark.*]

MAN. *Haai*, Sizwe! You are a country fool! Leading Mr Buntu and Mr Bansi astray. You think you know this place New Brighton? You know nothing!

[*Buntu comes running back.*]

BUNTU [*urgently*]. Let's get out of here.

MAN. Wait, Mr Buntu, I'm telling that fool Sizwe. . . .

BUNTU. Come on! There's trouble there . . . [*pointing in the direction from which he has come*] . . . let's move.

MAN. Wait, Mr Buntu, wait. Let me first tell that Sizwe. . . .

BUNTU. There's a dead man lying there!

MAN. Dead man?

BUNTU. I thought I was just pissing on a pile of rubbish, but when I looked carefully I saw it was a man. Dead. Covered in blood. Tsotsis must have got him. Let's get the hell out of here before anybody sees us.

MAN. Buntu . . . Buntu. . . .

BUNTU. Listen to me, Sizwe! The Tsotsis might still be around.

MAN. Buntu. . . .

BUNTU. Do you want to join him?

MAN. I don't want to join him.

BUNTU. Then come.

MAN. Wait, Buntu.

BUNTU. Jesus! If Zola had told me how much trouble you were going to be!

MAN. Buntu, ... we must report that man to the police station.

BUNTU. Police Station! Are you mad? You drunk, passbook not in order ... 'We've come to report a dead man, Sergeant.' 'Grab them!' Case closed. We killed him.

MAN. Mr Buntu, ... we can't leave him. ...

BUNTU. Please, Sizwe!

MAN. Wait. Let's carry him home.

BUNTU. Jst like that! Walk through New Brighton streets, at this hour, carrying a dead man. Anyway we don't know where he stays. Come.

MAN. Wait, Buntu, ... listen. ...

BUNTU. Sizwe!

MAN. Buntu, we can know where he stays. That passbook of his will talk. It talks, friend, like mine. His passbook will tell you.

BUNTU [after a moment's desperate hesitation]. You really want to land me in the shit, hey.
 Disappears into the dark again.]

MAN. It will tell you in good English where he stays. My passbook talks good English too ... big words that Sizwe can't read and doesn't understand. Sizwe wants to stay here in New Brighton and find a job; passbook says, 'No! Report back.'
Sizwe wants to feed his wife and children; passbook says, 'No. Endorsed out.'
Sizwe wants to. ...
 [Buntu reappears, a passbook in his hand. Looks around furtively and moves to the light under a lamp-post.]
They never told us it would be like that when they introduced it. They said: Book of Life! Your friend! You'll never get lost! They told us lies.
 [He joins Buntu who is examining the book.]

BUNTU. Haai! Look at him [the photograph in the book, reading]. 'Robert Zwelinzima. Tribe: Xhosa. Native Identification Number. ...'

MAN. Where does he stay, Buntu?

BUNTU [*paging through the book*]. Worked at Dorman Long seven years . . . Kilomet Engineering . . . eighteen months . . . Anderson Hardware two years . . . now unemployed. Hey, look, Sizwe! He's one up on you. He's got a work-seeker's permit.

MAN. Where does he stay, Buntu?

BUNTU. Lodger's Permit at 42 Mdala Street. From there to Sangocha Street . . . now at. . . .

[*Pause. Closes the book abruptly.*]

To hell with it I'm not going *there*.

MAN. Where, Buntu?

BUNTU [*emphatically*]. I Am Not Going There!

MAN. Buntu. . . .

BUNTU. You know where he is staying now? Single Men's Quarters! If you think I'm going there this time of the night you got another guess coming.

[*Sizwe doesn't understand.*]

Look, Sizwe . . . I stay in a house, there's a street name and a number. Easy to find. Ask anybody . . . Mapija Street? That way. You know what Single Men's Quarters is? Big bloody concentration camp with rows of things that look like train carriages. Six doors to each! Twelve people behind each door! You want me to go there now? Knock on the first one: 'Does Robert Zwelinzima live here?' 'No!' Next one: 'Does Robert . . . ?' 'Bugger off, we're trying to sleep!' Next one: 'Does Robert Zwelinzima . . . ?' They'll fuck us up, man! I'm putting this book back and we're going home.

MAN. Buntu!

BUNTU [*half-way back to the alleyway*]. What?

MAN. Would you do that to me, friend? If the Tsotsis had stabbed Sizwe, and left him lying there, would you walk away from him as well?

[*The accusation stops Buntu.*]

Would you leave me lying there, wet with your piss? I wish I was dead. I wish I was dead because I don't care a damn about anything any more.

[*Turning away from Buntu to the audience.*]

What's happening in this world, good people? Who cares for who in this world? Who wants who?

Who wants me, friend? What's wrong with me? I'm a man. I've got eyes to see. I've got ears to listen when people talk. I've got a head to think good things. What's wrong with me?

[*Starts to tear off his clothes.*]

Look at me! I'm a man. I've got legs. I can run with a wheelbarrow full of cement! I'm strong! I'm a man. Look! I've got a wife. I've got four children. How many has he made, lady? [*The man sitting next to her.*] Is he a man? What has he got that I haven't . . . ?

[*A thoughtful Buntu rejoins them, the dead man's reference book still in his hand.*]

BUNTU. Let me see your book?

[*Sizwe doesn't respond.*]

Give me your book!

MAN. Are you a policeman now, Buntu?

BUNTU. Give me your bloody book, Sizwe!

MAN [*handing it over*]. Take it, Buntu. Take this book and read it carefully, friend, and tell me what it says about me. Buntu, does that book tell you I'm a man?

[*Buntu studies the two books. Sizwe turns back to the audience.*]

That bloody book . . . ! People, do you know? No! Wherever you go . . . it's that bloody book. You go to school, it goes too. Go to work, it goes too. Go to church and pray and sing lovely hymns, it sits there with you. Go to hospital to die, it lies there too!

[*Buntu has collected Sizwe's discarded clothing.*]

BUNTU. Come!

[*Buntu's house, as earlier. Table and two chairs. Buntu pushes Sizwe down into a chair. Sizwe still muttering, starts to struggle back into his clothes. Buntu opens the two reference books and places them side by side on the table. He produces a pot of glue, then very carefully tears out the photograph in each book. A dab of glue on the back of each and then Sizwe's goes back into Robert's book, and Robert's into Sizwe's. Sizwe watches this operation, at first uninterestedly, but when he realizes what Buntu is up to, with growing*] *alarm. When he is finished, Buntu pushes the two books in front of Sizwe.*]

MAN [*shaking his head emphatically*]. *Yo! Haai, haai.* No, Buntu.

BUNTU. It's a chance.

MAN. *Haai, haai, haai* . . .

BUNTU. It's your only chance!

MAN. No, Buntu! What's it mean? That me, Sizwe Bansi. . . .

BUNTU. Is dead.

MAN. I'm not dead, friend.

BUNTU. We burn this book . . . [*Sizwe's original*] . . . and Sizwe Bansi disappears off the face of the earth.

MAN. What about the man we left lying in the alleyway?

BUNTU. Tomorrow the Flying Squad passes there and finds him. Check in his pockets . . . no passbook. Mount Road Mortuary. After three days nobody has identified him. Pauper's Burial. Case closed.

MAN. And then?

BUNTU. Tomorrow I contact my friend Norman at Feltex. He's a boss-boy there. I tell him about another friend, Robert Zwelinzima, book in order, who's looking for a job. You roll up later, hand over the book to the white man. Who does Robert Zwelinzima look like? You! Who gets the pay on Friday? You, man!

MAN. What about all that shit at the Labour Bureau, Buntu?

BUNTU. You don't have to there. This chap had a work-seeker's permit, Sizwe. All you do is hand over the book to the white man. *He* checks at the Labour Bureau. They check with their big machine. 'Robert Zwelinzima has the right to be employed and stay in this town.'

MAN. I don't want to lose my name, Buntu.

BUNTU. You mean you don't want to lose your bloody passbook! You love it, hey?

MAN. Buntu. I cannot lose my name.

BUNTU [*leaving the table*]. All right, I was only trying to help. As Robert Zwelinzima you could have stayed and worked in this town. As Sizwe Bansi . . . ? Start walking, friend. King William's Town. Hundred and fifty miles. And don't waste any time!

You've got to be there by yesterday. Hope you enjoy it.

MAN. Buntu. . . .

BUNTU. Lots of scenery in a hundred and fifty miles.

MAN. Buntu! . . .

BUNTU. Maybe a better idea is just to wait until they pick you up. Save yourself all that walking. Into the train with the escort! Smart stuff, hey. Hope it's not too crowded though. Hell of a lot of people being kicked out, I hear.

MAN. Buntu! . . .

BUNTU. But once you're back! Sit down on the side of the road next to your pondok with your family . . . the whole Bansi clan on leave . . . for life! Hey, that sounds okay. Watching all the cars passing, and as you say, friend, cough your bloody lungs out with Ciskeian Independence.

MAN [now really desperate]. Buntu!!!

BUNTU. What you waiting for? Go!

MAN. Buntu.

BUNTU. What?

MAN. What about my wife, Nowetu?

BUNTU. What about her?

MAN [maudlin tears] Her loving husband, Siwze Bansi, is dead!

BUNTU. So what! She's going to marry a better man.

MAN [bridling]. Who?

BUNTU. You . . . Robert Zwelinzima.

MAN [thoroughly confused]. How can I marry my wife, Buntu?

BUNTU. Get her down here and I'll introduce you.

MAN. Don't make jokes, Buntu. Robert . . . Sizwe . . . I'm all mixed up. Who am I?

BUNTU. A fool who is not taking his chance.

MAN. And my children! Their father is Sizwe Bansi. They're registered at school under Bansi. . . .

BUNTU. Are you really worried about your children, friend, or are you just worried about yourself and your bloody name? Wake up, man! Use that book and with your pay on Friday you'll have a real chance to do something for them.

MAN. I'm afraid. How do I get used to Robert? How do I live as another man's ghost?

BUNTU. Wasn't Sizwe Bansi a ghost?

MAN. No!

BUNTU. No? When the white man looked at you at the Labour Bureau what did he see? A man with dignity or a bloody passbook with an N.I. number? Isn't that a ghost? When the white man sees you walk down the street and calls out, 'Hey, John! Come here' . . . to you, *Sizwe Bansi* . . . isn't that a ghost? Or when his little child calls you 'Boy' . . . you a man, circumcised with a wife and four children . . . isn't that a ghost? Stop fooling yourself. All I'm saying is be a real ghost, if that is what they want, what they've turned us into. Spook them into hell, man!

[*Sizwe is silenced. Buntu realizes his words are beginning to reach the other man. He paces quietly, looking for his next move. He finds it.*]

Suppose you try my plan. Friday. Roughcasting section at Feltex. Paytime. Line of men—non-skilled labourers. White man with the big box full of pay-packets.

'John Kani!' 'Yes, sir!' Pay-packet is handed over. 'Thank you, sir.'

Another one. [*Buntu reads the name on an imaginary pay-packet.*] 'Winston Ntshona!' 'Yes, sir!' Pay-packet over. 'Thank you, sir!' Another one. 'Fats Bhokolane!' '*Hier is ek, my baas!*' Pay-packet over. '*Dankie, my baas!*'

Another one. 'Robert Zwelinzima!'

[*No response from Sizwe.*]

'Robert Zwelinzima!'

MAN. Yes, sir.

BUNTU [*handing him the imaginary pay-packet*]. Open it. Go on.

[*Takes back the packet, tears it open, empties its contents on the table, and counts it.*]

Five . . . ten . . . eleven . . . twelve . . . and ninety-nine cents. In *your* pocket!

[*Buntu again paces quietly, leaving Sizwe to think. Eventually. . . .*]

Saturday. Man in overalls, twelve rand ninety-nine cents

38

in the back pocket, walking down Main Street looking for Sales House. Finds it and walks in. Salesman comes forward to meet him.

'I've come to buy a suit.' Salesman is very friendly.

'Certainly. Won't you take a seat. I'll get the forms. I'm sure you want to open an account, sir. Six months to pay. But first I'll need all your particulars.'

[*Buntu has turned the table, with Sizwe on the other side, into the imaginary scene at Sales House.*]

BUNTU [*pencil poised, ready to fill in a form*]. Your name, please, sir?

MAN [*playing along uncertainly*]. Robert Zwelinzima.

BUNTU [*writing*]. 'Robert Zwelinzima.' Address?

MAN. Fifty, Mapija Street.

BUNTU. Where do you work?

MAN. Feltex.

BUNTU. And how much do you get paid?

MAN. Twelve . . . twelve rand ninety-nine cents.

BUNTU. N.I. Number, please?

[*Sizwe hesitates.*]

Your Native Identity number please?

[*Sizwe is still uncertain. Buntu abandons the act and picks up Robert Zwelinzima's passbook. He reads out the number.*]

N—I—3—8—1—1—8—6—3.

Burn that into your head, friend. You hear me? It's more important than your name.

N.I. number . . . three. . . .

MAN. Three.

BUNTU. Eight.

MAN. Eight.

BUNTU. One.

MAN. One.

BUNTU. One.

MAN. One.

BUNTU. Eight.

MAN. Eight.

BUNTU. Six.

MAN. Six.

BUNTU. Three.

MAN. Three.

BUNTU. Again. Three.

MAN. Three.

BUNTU. Eight.

MAN. Eight.

BUNTU. One.

MAN. One.

BUNTU. One.

MAN. One.

BUNTU. Eight.

MAN. Eight.

BUNTU. Six.

MAN. Six.

BUNTU. Three.

MAN. Three.

BUNTU [*picking up his pencil and returning to the role of the salesman*]. N.I. number, please.

MAN [*pausing frequently, using his hands to remember*]. Three . . . eight . . . one . . . one . . . eight . . . six . . . three. . . .

BUNTU [*abandoning the act*]. Good boy.

[*He paces. Sizwe sits and waits.*]

Sunday. Man in a Sales House suit, hat on top, going to church. Hymn book and bible under the arm. Sits down in the front pew. Priest in the pulpit.

[*Buntu jumps on to a chair in his new role. Sizwe kneels.*]

The Time has come!

MAN. Amen!

BUNTU. Pray, brothers and sisters. . . . Pray. . . . Now!

MAN. Amen.

BUNTU. The Lord wants to save you. Hand yourself over to

him, while there is still time, while Jesus is still prepared to listen to you.

MAN [*carried away by what he is feeling*]. Amen, Jesus!

BUNTU. Be careful, my brothers and sisters. . . .

MAN. Hallelujah!

BUNTU. Be careful lest when the big day comes and the pages of the big book are turned, it is found that your name is missing. Repent before it is too late.

MAN. Hallelujah! Amen.

BUNTU. Will all those who have not yet handed in their names for membership of our burial society please remain behind.

[*Buntu leaves the pulpit and walks around with a register.*]

Name, please, sir? Number? Thank you.

Good afternoon, sister. Your name, please.

Address? Number? God bless you.

[*He has reached Sizwe.*]

Your name, please, brother?

MAN. Robert Zwelinzima.

BUNTU. Address?

MAN. Fifty, Mapija Street.

BUNTU. N.I. number.

MAN [*again tremendous effort to remember*]. Three . . . eight . . . one . . . one . . . eight . . . six . . . three. . . .

[*They both relax.*]

BUNTU [*after pacing for a few seconds*]. Same man leaving the church . . . walking down the street.

[*Buntu acts out the role while Sizwe watches. He greets other members of the congregation.*]

'God bless you, Brother Bansi. May you always stay within the Lord's mercy.'

'Greetings, Brother Bansi. We welcome you into the flock of Jesus with happy spirits.'

'God bless you, Brother Bansi. Stay with the Lord, the Devil is strong.'

Suddenly. . . .

[*Buntu has moved to behind Sizwe. He grabs him roughly by the shoulder.*]

Police!

[*Sizwe stands up frightened. Buntu watches him carefully.*]

No, man! Clean your face.

[*Sizwe adopts an impassive expression. Buntu continues as the policeman.*]

What's your name?

MAN. Robert Zwelinzima.

BUNTU. Where do you work?

MAN. Feltex.

BUNTU. Book!

[*Sizwe hands over the book and waits while the policeman opens it, looks at the photograph, then Sizwe, and finally checks through its stamps and endorsements. While all this is going on Sizwe stands quietly, looking down at his feet, whistling under his breath. The book is finally handed back.*]

Okay.

[*Sizwe takes his book and sits down.*]

MAN [*after a pause*]. I'll try it, Buntu.

BUNTU. Of course you must, if you want to stay alive.

MAN. Yes, but Sizwe Bansi is dead.

BUNTU. What about Robert Zwelinzima then? That poor bastard I pissed on out there in the dark. So *he's* alive again. Bloody miracle, man.
Look, if someone was to offer me the things I wanted most in my life, the things that would make me, my wife, and my child happy, in exchange for the name Buntu . . . you think I wouldn't swop?

MAN. Are you sure, Buntu?

BUNTU [*examining the question seriously*]. If there was just me . . . I mean, if I was alone, if I didn't have anyone to worry about or look after except myself . . . maybe then I'd be prepared to pay some sort of price for a little pride. But if I had a wife and four children wasting away their one and only life in the dust and poverty of Ciskeian Independence . . . if I had four children waiting for me, their father, to do something about their lives . . . *ag*, no, Sizwe. . . .

MAN. Robert, Buntu.

BUNTU [*angry*]. All right! Robert, John, Athol, Winston. . . . Shit on names, man! To hell with them if in exchange you can get a piece of bread for your stomach and a blanket in winter. Understand me, brother, I'm not saying that pride isn't a way for us. What I'm saying is shit on our pride if we only bluff ourselves that we are men.

Take your name back, Sizwe Bansi, if it's so important to you. But next time you hear a white man say 'John' to you, don't say '*Ja, Baas?*' And next time the bloody white man says to you, a man, 'Boy, come here,' don't run to him and lick his arse like we all do. Face him and tell him: 'White man. I'm a Man!' *Ag kak!* We're bluffing ourselves.

It's like my father's hat. Special hat, man! Carefully wrapped in plastic on top of the wardrobe in his room. God help the child who so much as touches it! Sunday it goes on his head, and a man, full of dignity, a man I respect, walks down the street. White man stops him: 'Come here, kaffir!' What does he do?

[*Buntu whips the imaginary hat off his head and crumples it in his hands as he adopts a fawning, servile pose in front of the white man.*]

'What is it, Baas?'

If that is what you call pride, then shit on it! Take mine and give me food for my children.

[*Pause.*]

Look, brother, Robert Zwelinzima, that poor bastard out there in the alleyway, if there *are* ghosts, he is smiling tonight. He is here, with us, and he's saying: 'Good luck, Sizwe! I hope it works.' He's a brother, man.

MAN. For how long, Buntu?

BUNTU. How long? For as long as you can stay out of trouble. Trouble will mean police station, then fingerprints off to Pretoria to check on previous convictions . . . and when they do that . . . Siswe Bansi will live again and you will have had it.

MAN. Buntu, you know what you are saying? A black man stay out of trouble? Impossible, Buntu. Our skin is trouble.

BUNTU [*wearily*]. You said you wanted to try.

MAN. And I will.

BUNTU [*picks up his coat*]. I'm tired, . . . Robert. Good luck. See you tomorrow.

[*Exit Buntu, Sizwe picks up the passbook, looks at it for a long time, then puts it in his back pocket. He finds his walking-stick, newspaper, and pipe and moves downstage into a solitary light. He finishes the letter to his wife.*]

MAN. So Nowetu, for the time being my troubles are over. Christmas I come home. In the meantime Buntu is working a plan to get me a Lodger's Permit. If I get it, you and the children can come here and spend some days with me in Port Elizabeth. Spend the money I am sending you carefully. If all goes well I will send some more each week.

I do not forget you, my dear wife.

Your loving Husband,
Sizwe Bansi.

[*As he finishes the letter, Sizwe returns to the pose of the photo. Styles Photographic Studio. Styles is behind the camera.*]

STYLES. Hold it, Robert. Hold it just like that. Just one more. Now smile, Robert. . . . Smile. . . . Smile. . . .

[*Camera flash and blackout.*]

THE ISLAND

devised by

ATHOL FUGARD, JOHN KANI, AND WINSTON NTSHONA

CHARACTERS

JOHN
WINSTON   (two prisoners)

This play was given its first performance on 2 July 1973, directed by Athol Fugard with John Kani as John and Winston Ntshona as Winston.

SCENE ONE

Centre stage: a raised area representing a cell on Robben Island. Blankets and sleeping-mats—the prisoners sleep on the floor—are neatly folded. In one corner are a bucket of water and two tin mugs.

The long drawn-out wail of a siren. Stage-lights come up to reveal a moat of harsh, white light around the cell. In it the two prisoners—John stage-right and Winston stage-left—mime the digging of sand. They wear the prison uniform of khaki shirt and short trousers. Their heads are shaven. It is an image of back-breaking and grotesquely futile labour. Each in turns fills a wheelbarrow and then with great effort pushes it to where the other man is digging, and empties it. As a result, the piles of sand never diminish. Their labour is interminable. The only sounds are their grunts as they dig, the squeal of the wheel-barrows as they circle the cell, and the hum of Hodoshe, the green carrion fly.

A whistle is blown. They stop digging and come together, standing side by side as they are handcuffed together and shackled at the ankles. Another whistle. They start to run . . . John mumbling a prayer, Winston muttering a rhythm for their three-legged run.

They do not run fast enough. They get beaten . . . Winston receiving a bad blow to the eye and John spraining an ankle. In this condition they arrive finally at the cell door. Handcuffs and shackles are taken off. After being searched, they lurch into their cell. The door closes behind them. Both men sink to the floor.

A moment of total exhaustion until slowly, painfully, they start to explore their respective injuries . . . Winston his eye, and John his ankle. Winston is moaning softly and this eventually draws John's attention away from his ankle. He crawls to Winston and examines the injured eye. It needs attention. Winston's moaning is slowly turning into a sound of inarticulate outrage, growing in volume and violence. John urinates into one hand and tries to clean the other man's eye with it, but Winston's anger and outrage are now uncontrollable. He breaks away from John and crawls around the cell, blind with rage and pain. John tries to placate him . . . the noise could bring back the warders and still more trouble. Winston eventually finds the cell door but before he can start banging on it John pulls him away.

WINSTON [*calling*]. Hodoshe!

JOHN. Leave him, Winston. Listen to me, man! If he comes now we'll be in bigger shit.

47

WINSTON. I want Hodoshe. I want him now! I want to take him to the office. He must read my warrant. I was sentenced to Life brother, not bloody Death!

JOHN. Please, Winston! He made us run. . . .

WINSTON. I want Hodoshe!

JOHN. He made us run. He's happy now. Leave him. Maybe he'll let us go back to the quarry tomorrow. . . .

[*Winston is suddenly silent. For a moment John thinks his words are having an effect, but then he realizes that the other man is looking at his ear. Winston touches it. It is bleeding. A sudden spasm of fear from John who puts a hand to his ear. His fingers come away with blood on them. The two men look at each other.*]

WINSTON. *Nyana we Sizwe!*

[*In a reversal of earlier roles Winston now gets John down on the floor of the cell so as to examine the injured ear. He has to wipe blood and sweat out of his eyes in order to see clearly. John winces with pain. Winston keeps restraining him.*]

WINSTON [*eventually*]. It's not too bad. [*Using his shirt-tail he cleans the injured ear.*]

JOHN [*through clenched teeth as Winston tends his ear*]. Hell, *ons was gemoer vandag!* [*A weak smile.*] News bulletin and weather forecast! Black Domination was chased by White Domination. Black Domination lost its shoes and collected a few bruises. Black Domination will run barefoot to the quarry tomorrow. Conditions locally remain unchanged—thunderstorms with the possibility of cold showers and rain. Elsewhere, fine and warm!

[*Winston has now finished tending John's ear and settles down on the floor beside him. He clears his nose, ears, and eyes of sand.*]

WINSTON. Sand! Same old sea sand I used to play with when I was young. St George's Strand. New Year's Day. Sand dunes. Sand castles. . . .

JOHN. *Ja*, we used to go there too. Last. . . . [*Pause and then a small laugh. He shakes his head.*] The Christmas before they arrested me, we were down there. All of us. Honeybush. My little Monde played in the sand. We'd given her one of those little buckets and spades for Christmas.

WINSTON. *Ja.*

JOHN. Anyway, it was Daddy's turn today. [*Shaking his head ruefully.*] *Haai*, Winston, this one goes on the record. 'Struesgod! I'm a man, brother. A man! But if Hodoshe had kept us at those wheelbarrows five minutes longer . . . ! There would have been a baby on the Island tonight. I nearly cried.

WINSTON. *Ja*.

JOHN. There was no end to it, except one of us!

WINSTON. That's right.

JOHN. This morning when he said: 'You two! The beach!' . . . I thought, Okay, so it's my turn to empty the sea into a hole. He likes that one. But when he pointed to the wheelbarrows, and I saw his idea . . . ! [*Shaking his head.*] I laughed at first. Then I wasn't laughing. Then I hated you. You looked so stupid, *broer!*

WINSTON. That's what he wanted.

JOHN. It was going to last forever, man! Because of *you*. And for *you*, because of *me*. *Moer!* He's cleverer than I thought.

WINSTON. If he was God, he would have done it.

JOHN. What?

WINSTON. Broken us. Men get tired. Hey! There's a thought. We're still alive because Hodoshe got tired.

JOHN. Tomorrow?

WINSTON. We'll see.

JOHN. If he takes us back there . . . If I hear that wheelbarrow . . . of yours again, coming with another bloody load of . . . eternity!

WINSTON [*with calm resignation*]. We'll see.

[*Pause. John looks at Winston.*]

JOHN [*with quiet emphasis, as if the other man did not fully understand the significance of what he had said*]. I *hated* you Winston.

WINSTON [*meeting John's eyes*]. *I* hated *you*.

[*John puts a hand on Winston's shoulder. Their brotherhood is intact. He gets slowly to his feet.*]

JOHN. Where's the *lap?*

WINSTON. Somewhere. Look for it.

JOHN. Hey! You had it last.

[*Limping around the cell looking for their washrag.*]

WINSTON. *Haai*, man! You got no wife here. Look for the rag yourself.

JOHN [*finding the rag beside the water bucket*]. Look where it is. Look! Hodoshe comes in here and sees it. 'Whose *lappie* is that?' Then what do you say?

WINSTON. 'It's his rag, sir.'

JOHN. Yes? Okay. 'It's my rag, sir.' When you wash, use your shirt.

WINSTON. Okay, okay! 'It's our rag, sir!'

JOHN. That will be the bloody day!

[*John, getting ready to wash, starts to take off his shirt. Winston produces a cigarette butt, matches, and flint from their hiding-place under the water bucket. He settles down for a smoke.*]

Shit, today was long. Hey, Winston, suppose the watch of the chap behind the siren is slow! We could still be there, man! [*He pulls out three or four rusty nails from a secret pocket in his trousers. He holds them out to Winston.*] Hey there.

WINSTON. What?

JOHN. With the others.

WINSTON [*taking the nails*]. What's this?

JOHN. Necklace, man. With the others.

WINSTON. Necklace?

JOHN. Antigone's necklace.

WINSTON. *Ag*, shit, man!

[*Slams the nails down on the cell floor and goes on smoking.*]

Antigone! Go to hell, man, John.

JOHN. Hey, don't start any nonsense now. You promised. [*Limps over to Winston's bed-roll and produces a half-completed necklace made of nails and string.*] It's nearly finished. Look. Three fingers, one nail . . . three fingers, one nail. . . . [*Places the necklace beside Winston who is shaking his head, smoking aggressively, and muttering away.*] Don't start any nonsense now, Winston. There's six days to go to the concert. We're committed. We promised the chaps we'd do something. This *Antigone* is just right for us. Six more days and we'll make it.

[*He continues washing.*]

WINSTON. Jesus, John! We were down on the beach today. Hodoshe made us run. Can't you just leave a man . . . ?

JOHN. To hell with you! Who do you think ran with you? I'm also tired, but we can't back out now. Come on! Three fingers. . . .

WINSTON. . . . one nail! [*Shaking his head.*] *Haai . . . haai . . . haai!*

JOHN. Stop moaning and get on with it. Shit, Winston! What sort of progress is this? [*Abandoning his wash.*] Listen. Listen! Number 42 is practising the Zulu War Dance. Down there they're rehearsing their songs. It's just in this *moer* cell that there's always an argument. Today you want to do it, tomorrow you don't want to do it. How the hell must I know what to report to the chaps tomorrow if we go back to the quarry?

[*Winston is unyielding. His obstinacy gets the better of John, who eventually throws the wash-rag at him.*]

There! Wash!

[*John applies himself to the necklace while Winston, still muttering away in an undertone, starts to clean himself.*]

How can I be sure of anything when you carry on like this? We've still got to learn the words, the moves. Shit! It could be so bloody good, man.

[*Winston mutters protests all the way through this speech of John's. The latter holds up the necklace.*]

Nearly finished! Look at it! Three fingers. . . .

WINSTON. . . . one nail.

JOHN. *Ja!* Simple. Do you still remember all I told you yesterday? Bet you've bloody forgotten. How can I carry on like this? I can't move on, man. Over the whole bloody lot again! Who Antigone is . . . who Creon is. . . .

WINSTON. Antigone is mother to Polynices. . . .

JOHN. *Haai, haai, haai* . . . shit, Winston! [*Now really exasperated.*] How many times must I tell you that Antigone is the sister to the two brothers? Not the mother. That's another play.

WINSTON. Oh.

JOHN. That's all you know! 'Oh.' [*He abandons the necklace and fishes out a piece of chalk from a crack in the floor.*] Come here. This is the last time. 'Struesgod. The last time.

WINSTON. *Ag*, no, John.

JOHN. Come! I'm putting this plot down for the last time! If you don't learn it tonight I'm going to report you to the old men tomorrow. And remember, *broer*, those old men will make Hodoshe and his tricks look like a little boy.

WINSTON. Jesus Christ! Learn to dig for Hodoshe, learn to run for Hodoshe, and what happens when I get back to the cell? Learn to read *Antigone!*

JOHN. Come! And shut up! [*He pulls the reluctant Winston down beside him on the floor. Winston continues to clean himself with the rag while John lays out the 'plot' of Antigone.*] If you would just stop moaning, you would learn faster. Now listen!

WINSTON. Okay, do it.

JOHN. Listen! It is the Trial of Antigone. Right?

WINSTON. So you say.

JOHN. First, the accused. Who is the accused?

WINSTON. Antigone.

JOHN. Coming from you that's bloody progress. [*Writing away on the cell floor with his chalk.*] Next the State. Who is the State?

WINSTON. Creon.

JOHN. King Creon. Creon is the State. Now . . . what did Antigone do?

WINSTON. Antigone buried her brother Eteocles.

JOHN. No, no, no! Shit, Winston, when are you going to remember this thing? I told you, man, Antigone buried Polynices. The traitor! The one who I said was on *our* side. Right?

WINSTON. Right.

JOHN. Stage one of the Trial. [*Writing on the floor.*] The State lays its charges against the Accused . . . and lists counts . . . you know the way they do it. Stage two is Pleading. What does Antigone plead? Guilty or Not Guilty?

WINSTON. Not Guilty.

JOHN [*trying to be tactful*]. Now look, Winston, we're not going to argue. Between me and you, in this cell, we know she's

Not Guilty. But in the play she pleads Guilty.

WINSTON. No, man, John! Antigone is Not Guilty. . . .

JOHN. In the play. . . .

WINSTON [*losing his temper*]. To hell with the play! Antigone had every right to bury her brother.

JOHN. Don't say 'To hell with the play'. We've got to do the bloody thing. And in the play she pleads Guilty. Get that straight. Antigone pleads. . . .

WINSTON [*giving up in disgust*]. Okay, do it your way.

JOHN. It's not my way! In the play. . . .

WINSTON. Guilty!

JOHN. Yes, Guilty!

[*Writes furiously on the floor.*]

WINSTON. Guilty.

JOHN. Stage three, Pleading in Mitigation of Sentence. Stage four, Sentence, State Summary, and something from you . . . Farewell Words. Now learn that.

WINSTON. Hey?

JOHN [*getting up*]. Learn that!

WINSTON. But we've just done it!

JOHN. *I've* just done it. Now *you* learn it.

WINSTON [*throwing aside the wash-rag with disgust before applying himself to learning the 'plot'*]. Learn to run, learn to read. . . .

JOHN. And don't throw the rag there! [*Retrieving the rag and placing it in its correct place.*] Don't be so bloody difficult, man. We're nearly there. You'll be proud of this thing when we've done it.

[*Limps to his bed-roll and produces a pendant made from a jam-tin lid and twine.*] Look. Winston, look! Creon's medallion. Good, hey! [*Hangs it around his neck.*] I'll finish the necklace while you learn that.

[*He strings on the remaining nails.*] Jesus, Winston! June 1965.

WINSTON. What?

JOHN. This, man. *Antigone*. In New Brighton. St. Stephen's Hall. The place was packed, man! All the big people. Front row . . . dignitaries. Shit, those were the days. Georgie was Creon. You know Georgie?

WINSTON. The teacher?

JOHN. That's him. He played Creon. Should have seen him, Winston. Short and fat, with big eyes, but by the time the play was finished he was as tall as the roof.

[*Onto his legs in an imitation of Georgie's Creon.*]

'My Councillors, now that the Gods have brought our City safe through a storm of troubles to tranquillity. . . .' And old Mulligan! Another short-arsed teacher. With a beard! He used to go up to the Queen. . . . [*Another imitation.*] 'Your Majesty, prepare for grief, but do not weep.'

[*The necklace in his hands.*]

Nearly finished!

Nomhle played Antigone. A bastard of a lady that one, but a beautiful bitch. Can't get her out of my mind tonight.

WINSTON [*indicating the 'plot'*]. I know this.

JOHN. You sure?

WINSTON. This! . . . it's here. [*Tapping his head.*]

JOHN. You're not bullshitting, hey? [*He rubs out the 'plot' and then paces the cell.*] Right. The Trial of Antigone. Who is the Accused?

WINSTON. Antigone.

JOHN. Who is the State?

WINSTON. King Creon.

JOHN. Stage one.

WINSTON [*supremely self-confident*]. Antigone lays charges. . . .

JOHN. NO, SHIT, MAN, WINSTON!!!

[*Winston pulls John down and stifles his protests with a hand over his mouth.*]

WINSTON. Okay . . . okay . . . listen, John . . . listen. . . . The State lays charges against Antigone.

[*Pause.*]

JOHN. Be careful!

WINSTON. The State lays charges against Antigone.

JOHN. Stage two.

WINSTON. Pleading.

JOHN. What does she plead? Guilty or Not Guilty?

WINSTON. Guilty.

JOHN. Stage three.

WINSTON. Pleading in Mitigation of Sentence.

JOHN. Stage four.

WINSTON. State Summary, Sentence, and Farewell Words.

JOHN [*very excited*]. He's got it! That's my man. See how easy it is, Winston? Tomorrow, just the words.

[*Winston gets onto his legs, John puts away the props. Mats and blankets are unrolled. The two men prepare for sleep.*]

JOHN. Hell, I hope we go back to the quarry tomorrow. There's still a lot of things we need for props and costumes. Your wig! The boys in Number Fourteen said they'd try and smuggle me a piece of rope from the jetty.

WINSTON. *Ja*, I hope we're back there. I want to try and get some tobacco through to Sipho.

JOHN. Sipho?

WINSTON. Back in solitary.

JOHN. Again!

WINSTON. *Ja*.

JOHN. Oh hell!

WINSTON. Simon passed the word.

JOHN. What was it this time?

WINSTON. Complained about the food I think. Demanded to see the book of Prison Regulations.

JOHN. Why don't they leave him alone for a bit?

WINSTON. Because he doesn't leave them alone.

JOHN. You're right. I'm glad I'm not in Number Twenty-two with him. One man starts getting hard-arsed like that and the whole lot of you end up in the shit.

[*Winston's bed is ready. He lies down.*]

You know what I'm saying?

WINSTON. *Ja*.

JOHN. What?

WINSTON. What 'What'?

JOHN. What am I saying?

WINSTON. *Haai*, Johnny, man! I'm tired now! Let a man. . . .

JOHN. I'm saying Don't Be Hard-Arsed! You! When Hodoshe opens that door tomorrow say '*Ja, Baas*' the right way. I don't want to be back on that bloody beach tomorrow just because you feel like being difficult.

WINSTON [*wearily*]. Okay, man, Johnny.

JOHN. You're not alone in this cell. I'm here too.

WINSTON. Jesus, you think I don't know that!

JOHN. People must remember their responsibilities to others.

WINSTON. I'm glad to hear you say that, because I was just going to remind you that it is your turn tonight.

JOHN. What do you mean? Wasn't it my turn last night?

WINSTON [*shaking his head emphatically*]. *Haai, haai.* Don't you remember? Last night I took you to bioscope.

JOHN. Hey, by the way! So you did. Bloody good film too. 'Fastest Gun in the West'. Glenn Ford.

[*Whips out a six-shooter and guns down a few bad-men.*]

You were bullshitting me a bit though. How the hell can Glenn Ford shoot backwards through his legs. I tried to work that one out on the beach.

[*He is now seated on his bed-roll. After a moment's thought he holds up an empty mug as a telephone-receiver and starts to dial. Winston watches him with puzzlement.*]

Operator, put me through to New Brighton, please . . . yes, New Brighton, Port Elizabeth. The number is 414624. . . . Yes, mine is local . . . local. . . .

WINSTON [*recognizing the telephone number*]. The Shop!

[*He sits upright with excitement as John launches into the telephone conversation.*]

JOHN. That you Scott? Hello, man! Guess who! . . . You got it! You bastard! Hell, shit, Scott, man . . . how things with you? No, still inside. Give me the news, man . . . you don't say! No, we don't hear anything here . . . not a word. . . . What's that? Business is bad? . . . You bloody undertaker! People aren't dying fast enough! No, things are fine here. . . .

[*Winston, squirming with excitement, has been trying unsuccessfully to interrupt John's torrent of words and laughter. He finally succeeds in drawing John's attention.*]

WINSTON. Who else is there? Who's with Scott?

JOHN. Hey, Scott, who's there with you? . . . Oh no! . . . call him to the phone, man. . . .

WINSTON. Who's it?

JOHN [*ignoring Winston*]. Just for a minute, man, please, Scott. . . .

[*Ecstatic response from John as another voice comes over the phone.*]

Hello there, you beautiful bastard . . . how's it, man? . . .

WINSTON. Who the hell is it, man?

JOHN [*hand over the receiver*]. Sky!

[*Winston can no longer contain his excitement. He scrambles out of his bed to join John, and joins in the fun with questions and remarks whispered into John's ear. Both men enjoy it enormously.*]

How's it with Mangi? Where's Vusi? How are the chaps keeping, Sky? Winston? . . . All right, man. He's here next to me. No, fine, man, fine, man . . . small accident today when he collided with Hodoshe, but nothing to moan about. His right eye bruised, that's all. Hey, Winston's asking how are the punkies doing? [*Big laugh.*] You bloody lover boy! Leave something for us, man!

[*John becomes aware of Winston trying to interrupt again: to Winston.*]

Okay . . . okay. . . .

[*Back to the telephone.*] Listen, Sky, Winston says if you get a chance, go down to Dora Street, to his wife. Tell V. Winston says he's okay, things are fine. Winston says she must carry on . . . nothing has happened . . . tell her to take care of everything and everybody. . . . *Ja.* . . .

[*The mention of his wife guillotines Winston's excitement and fun. After a few seconds of silence he crawls back heavily to his bed and lies down. A similar shift in mood takes place in John.*]

And look, Sky, you're not far from Gratten Street. Cross over to it, man, drop in on number thirty-eight, talk to Princess, my wife. How is she keeping? Ask her for me. I haven't received a letter for three months now. Why aren't they writing? Tell her to write, man. I want to know how the children are keeping. Is Monde still at school? How's my twin baby, my Father and Mother? Is the old girl sick? They mustn't be afraid to tell me. I want to know. I know it's an effort to write, but it means a lot to us here. Tell her . . . this was another day. They're not very different here. We were down on the beach. The wind was blowing. The sand got in our eyes. The sea was rough. I couldn't see the mainland properly. Tell them that maybe tomorrow we'll go to the quarry. It's not so bad there. We'll be with the others. Tell her also . . . it's starting to get cold now, but the worst is still coming.

[*Slow fade to blackout.*]

SCENE TWO

The cell, a few days later.
John is hidden under a blanket. Winston is in the process of
putting on Antigone's wig and false breasts.

JOHN. Okay?

WINSTON [*still busy*]. No.

JOHN. Okay?

WINSTON. No.

JOHN. Okay?

WINSTON. No.

[*Pause*]

JOHN. Okay?

[*Winston is ready. He stands waiting. John slowly lifts the blanket
and looks. He can't believe his eyes. Winston is a very funny sight.
John's amazement turns into laughter, which builds steadily. He
bangs on the cell wall.*]

Hey, Norman. Norman! Come this side, man. I got it here.
Poes!

[*John launches into an extravagant send-up of Winston's Antigone.
He circles 'her' admiringly, he fondles her breasts, he walks arm in
arm with her down Main Street, collapsing with laughter between
each 'turn'. He climaxes everything by dropping his trousers.*]

Speedy Gonzales! Here I come!

[*This last joke is too much for Winston who has endured the
whole performance with mounting but suppressed anger. He tears off
the wig and breasts, throws them down on the cell floor, and storms
over to the water bucket where he starts to clean himself.*]

WINSTON. It's finished! I'm not doing it. Take your Antigone
and shove it up your arse!

JOHN [*trying to control himself*]. Wait, man. Wait. . . .

[*He starts laughing again.*]

WINSTON. There is nothing to wait for, my friend. I'm not
doing it.

JOHN. Please, Winston!

WINSTON. You can laugh as much as you like, my friend, but

just let's get one thing straight, I'm *not* doing Antigone. And in case you want to know why . . . I'm a man, not a bloody woman.

JOHN. When did I say otherwise?

WINSTON. What were you laughing at?

JOHN. I'm not laughing now.

WINSTON. What are you doing, crying?

[*Another burst of laughter from John.*]

There you go again, more laughing! Shit, man, you want me to go out there tomorrow night and make a bloody fool of myself? You think I don't know what will happen after that? Every time I run to the quarry . . . 'Nyah . . . nyah. . . . Here comes Antigone! . . . Help the poor lady! . . .' Well, you can go to hell with your Antigone.

JOHN. I wasn't laughing at you.

WINSTON. Then who were you laughing at? Who else was here that dressed himself as a lady and made a bloody fool of himself?

JOHN [*now trying very hard to placate the other man*]. Okay Winston, Okay! I'm not laughing any more.

WINSTON. You can go to hell with what you're saying.

JOHN. Look, Winston, try to understand, man, . . . this is Theatre.

WINSTON. You call laughing at me Theatre? Then go to hell with your Theatre!

JOHN. Please, Winston, just stop talking and listen to me.

WINSTON. No! You get this, brother, . . . I am not doing your Antigone! I would rather run the whole day for Hodoshe. At least I know where I stand with him. All *he* wants is to make me a 'boy' . . . not a bloody woman.

JOHN. Okay, okay. . . .

WINSTON. Nothing you can say. . . .

JOHN [*shouting the other man down*]. Will you bloody listen!

WINSTON [*throwing the wash-rag down violently*]. Okay. I'm listening.

JOHN. Sure I laughed. *Ja . . . I laughed.* But can I tell you why I laughed? I was preparing you for . . . stage fright! You think I don't know what I'm doing in this cell? This is preparation for stage fright! I know those bastards out there. When you get in front of them, sure they'll laugh . . . Nyah, nyah! . . . they'll laugh. But just remember this brother, nobody laughs forever! There'll come a time when they'll stop laughing, and that will be the time when our Antigone hits them with her words.

WINSTON. You're day-dreaming, John. Just get it into your head that I'm not doing Antigone. It's as simple as that.

JOHN [*realizing for the first time that Winston needs to be handled very carefully*]. Hey, Winston! Hold on there, man. We've only got one more day to go! They've given us the best spot in the programme. We end the show! You can't back out now.

WINSTON. You think I can't? Just wait and see.

JOHN. Winston! You want to get me into trouble? Is that what you want?

WINSTON. Okay, I won't back out.

JOHN [*delighted with his easy victory*]. That's my man!

WINSTON [*retrieving the wig and false breasts off the floor and slamming them into John's hands*]. Here's Antigone . . . take these titties and hair and play Antigone. I'm going to play Creon. Do you understand what I'm saying? Take your two titties. . . . I'll have my balls and play Creon. [*Turns his back on a flabbergasted John, fishes out a cigarette-butt and matches from under the water bucket, and settles down for a smoke.*]

JOHN [*after a stunned silence*]. You won't make it! I thought about that one days ago. It's too late now to learn Creon's words.

WINSTON [*smoking*]. I hate to say it, but that is just too bad. I am not doing Antigone.

[*John is now furious. After a moment's hesitation he stuffs on the wig and false breasts and confronts Winston.*]

JOHN. Look at me. Now laugh.

[*Winston tries, but the laugh is forced and soon dies away.*]

Go on.

[*Pause.*]

Go on laughing! Why did you stop? Must I tell you why?

Because behind all this rubbish is me, and you know it's me.
You think those bastards out there won't know it's you? Yes,
they'll laugh. But who cares about that as long as they laugh
in the beginning and listen at the end. That's all we want them
to do . . . listen at the end!

WINSTON. I don't care what you say John. I'm not doing
Antigone.

JOHN. Winston . . . you're being difficult. You promised. . . .

WINSTON. Go to hell, man. Only last night you tell me that
this Antigone is a bloody . . . what you call it . . . legend! A
Greek one at that. Bloody thing never even happened. Not
even history! Look, brother, I got no time for bullshit. Fuck
legends. Me? . . . I live my life here! I know why I'm here,
and it's history, not legends. I had my chat with a magistrate
in Cradock and now I'm here. Your Antigone is a child's play,
man.

JOHN. Winston! That's Hodoshe's talk.

WINSTON. You can go to hell with that one too.

JOHN. Hodoshe's talk, Winston! That's what he says all the
time. What he wants us to say all our lives. Our convictions,
our ideals . . . that's what he calls them . . . child's play. Everything we fucking do is 'child's play' . . . when we ran that whole
day in the sun and pushed those wheelbarrows, when we cry,
when we shit . . . child's play! Look, brother, . . . I've had
enough. No one is going to stop me doing Antigone. . . .

[*The two men break apart suddenly, drop their trousers, and stand
facing the wall with arms outstretched. Hodoshe calls John.*]
Yes, sir!
[*He then pulls up his trousers and leaves the cell. When he has
left, Winston pulls up his trousers and starts muttering with savage
satisfaction at the thought of John in Hodoshe's hands.*]

WINSTON. There he goes. Serves him right. I just hope Hodoshe
teaches him a lesson. Antigone is important! Antigone this!
Antigone that! Shit, man. Nobody can sleep in this bloody cell
because of all that bullshit. Polynices! Eteocles! The other
prisoners too. Nobody gets any peace and quiet because of
that bloody Antigone! I hope Hodoshe gives it to him.

[*He is now at the cell door. He listens, then moves over to the wig
on the floor and circles it. He finally picks it up. Moves back to*

*the cell door to make sure no one is coming. The water bucket gives
him an idea. He puts on the wig and, after some difficulty, manages
to see his reflection in the water. A good laugh, which he cuts off
abruptly. He moves around the cell trying out a few of Antigone's
poses. None of them work. He feels a fool. He finally tears off the
wig and throws it down on the floor with disgust.*]

Ag voetsek!

[*Hands in pockets he paces the cell with grim determination.*]
I'm not going to do it. And I'm going to tell him. When
he comes back. For once he must just shut that big bloody
mouth of his and listen. To me! I'm not going to argue, but
'struesgod that . . . !

[*The wig on the floor. He stamps on it.*]
Shit, man! If he wants a woman in the cell he must send for his
wife, and I don't give a damn how he does it. I didn't walk
with those men and burn my bloody passbook in front of that
police station, and have a magistrate send me here for life
so that he can dress me up like a woman and make a bloody
fool of me. I'm going to tell him. When he walks through
that door.

[*John returns. Winston is so involved in the problem of Antigone
that at first he does not register John's strangely vacant manner.*]

Listen, *broer*, I'm not trying to be difficult but this Antigone!
No! Please listen to me, John. 'Struesgod I can't do it. I mean,
let's try something else, like singing or something. You always
got ideas. You know I can sing or dance. But not Antigone.
Please, John.

JOHN [*quietly*]. Winston. . . .

WINSTON [*still blind to the other man's manner*]. Don't let's argue,
man. We've been together in this cell too long now to quarrel
about rubbish. But you know me. If there's one thing I can't
stand it's people laughing at me. If I go out there tomorrow
night and those bastards start laughing I'll fuck up the first
one I lay my hands on. You saw yourself what happened
in here when you started laughing. I wanted to *moer* you,
John. I'm not joking. I really wanted to. . . . Hey, are you
listening to me? [*Looking squarely at John.*]

JOHN. Winston . . . I've got something to tell you.

WINSTON [*registering John's manner for the first time*]. What's the matter? Hodoshe? What happened? Are we in shit? Solitary?

JOHN. My appeal was heard last Wednesday. Sentence reduced. I've got three months to go.

[*Long silence. Winston is stunned. Eventually. . . .*]

WINSTON. Three. . . .

JOHN. . . . months to go.

WINSTON. Three. . . .

JOHN. *Ja.* That's what Prinsloo said.

WINSTON. John!

[*Winston explodes with joy. The men embrace. They dance a jig in the cell. Winston finally tears himself away and starts to hammer on the cell walls so as to pass on the news to other prisoners.*]

Norman! Norman!! John. Three months to go. *Ja.* . . . Just been told. . . .

[*Winston's excitement makes John nervous. He pulls Winston away from the wall.*]

JOHN. Winston! Not yet, man. We'll tell them at the quarry tomorrow. Let me just live with it for a little while.

WINSTON. Okay okay. . . . How did it happen?

[*He pulls John down to the floor. They sit close together.*]

JOHN. Jesus, I'm so mixed up, man! *Ja* . . . the door opened and I saw Hodoshe. Ooo God, I said to myself. Trouble! Here we go again! All because of you and the noise you were making. Went down the corridor straight to Number Four . . . Solitary and Spare Diet!! But at the end, instead of turning right, we turned left into the main block, all the way through it to Prinsloo's office.

WINSTON. Prinsloo!

JOHN. I'm telling you. Prinsloo himself, man. We waited outside for a little bit, then Hodoshe pushed me in. Prinsloo was behind his desk, busy with some papers. He pulled out one and said to me: 'You are very lucky. Your lawyers have been working on your case. The sentence has been reduced from ten years, to three.'

WINSTON. What did Hodoshe say?

JOHN. Nothing. But he looked unhappy.

[*They laugh.*]

Hey, something else. Hodoshe let me walk back here by myself! He didn't follow me.

WINSTON. Of course. You are free.

JOHN. *Haai*, Winston, not yet. Those three months . . . ! Or suppose it's a trick.

WINSTON. What do you mean?

JOHN. Those bastards will do anything to break you. If the wheelbarrows and the quarry don't do it, they'll try something else. Remember that last visit of wives, when they lined up all the men on the other side. . . . 'Take a good look and say goodbye! Back to the cells!'

WINSTON. You say you saw Prinsloo?

JOHN. Prinsloo himself. Bastard didn't even stand up when I walked in. And by the way . . . I had to sign. *Ja!* I had to sign a form to say that I had been officially told of the result of my appeal . . . that I had three months to go. *Ja*. I signed!

WINSTON [*without the slightest doubt*]. It's three months, John.

JOHN [*relaxing and living with the reality for the first time*]. Hell, Winston, at the end of those three months, it will be three years together in this cell. Three years ago I stood in front of that magistrate at Kirkwood—bastard didn't even look at me: 'Ten years!' I watched ten years of my life drift away like smoke from a cigarette while he fidgeted and scratched his arse. That same night back in the prison van to the cells at Rooihel. First time we met!

WINSTON. *Ja*. We had just got back from our trial in Cradock.

JOHN. You, Temba, . . .

WINSTON. Sipho. . . .

JOHN. Hell, man!

WINSTON. First time we got close to each other was the next morning in the yard, when they lined us up for the vans. . . .

JOHN. And married us!

[*They lock left and right hands together to suggest handcuffs.*]

WINSTON. Who was that old man . . . remember him? . . . in the corner handcuffed to Sipho?

JOHN. Sipho?

WINSTON. *Ja*, the one who started the singing.

JOHN [*remembering*]. Peter. Tatu Peter.

WINSTON. That's him!

JOHN. Hell, it comes back now, man! Pulling through the big gates, wives and mothers running next to the vans, trying to say goodbye . . . all of us inside fighting for a last look through the window.

WINSTON [*shaking his head*]. Shit!

JOHN. Bet you've forgotten the song the old man started?

[*Winston tries to remember. John starts singing softly. It is one of the Defiance Campaign songs. Winston joins in.*]

WINSTON [*shaking his head ruefully*]. By the time we reach Humansdorp though, nobody was singing.

JOHN. Fuck singing. I wanted to piss. Hey! I had my one free hand on my balls, holding on. I'd made a mistake when we left the Rooihel. Drank a gallon of water thinking of those five hundred miles ahead. Jesus! There was the bucket in the corner! But we were packed in so tight, remember, we couldn't move. I tried to pull you but it was no bloody good. So I held on—Humansdorp, Storms River, Blaaukrantz . . . held on. But at Knysna, to hell with it, I let go!

[*Gesture to indicate the release of his bladder. Winston finds this enormously funny. John joins in.*]

You were also wet by then!

WINSTON. Never!

JOHN. Okay, let's say that by George nobody was dry. Remember the stop there?

WINSTON. *Ja*. I thought they were going to let us walk around a bit.

JOHN. Not a damn! Fill up with petrol and then on. Hey, but what about those locals, the Coloured prisoners, when we pulled away. Remember? Coming to their cell windows and shouting . . . 'Courage, Brothers! Courage!' After that . . . ! Jesus, I was tired. Didn't we fall asleep? Standing like that?

WINSTON. What do you mean standing? It was impossible to fall.

JOHN. Then the docks, the boat. . . . It was my first time on one. I had nothing to vomit up, but my God I tried.

WINSTON. What about me?

JOHN. Then we saw this place for the first time. It almost looked pretty, hey, with all the mist around it.

WINSTON. I was too sick to see anything, *broer*.

JOHN. Remember your words when we jumped off onto the jetty?

[*Pause. The two men look at each other.*]

Heavy words, Winston. You looked back at the mountains . . . 'Farewell Africa!' I've never forgotten them. That was three years ago.

WINSTON. And now, for you, it's three months to go.

[*Pause. The mood of innocent celebration has passed. John realizes what his good news means to the other man.*]

JOHN. To hell with everything. Let's go to bed.

[*Winston doesn't move. John finds Antigone's wig.*]

We'll talk about Antigone tomorrow.

[*John prepares for bed.*]

Hey, Winston! I just realized. My family! Princess and the children. Do you think they've been told? Jesus, man, maybe they're also saying . . . three months! Those three months are going to feel as long as the three years. Time passes slowly when you've got something . . . to wait for. . . .

[*Pause. Winston still hasn't moved. John changes his tone.*]

Look, in this cell we're going to forget those three months. The whole bloody thing is most probably a trick anyway. So let's just forget about it. We run to the quarry tomorrow. Together. So let's sleep.

SCENE THREE

The cell, later the same night. Both men are in bed. Winston is apparently asleep. John, however, is awake, rolling restlessly from side to side. He eventually gets up and goes quietly to the bucket for a drink of water, then back to his bed. He doesn't lie down, however. Pulling the blanket around his shoulders he starts to think about the three months. He starts counting the days on the fingers of one hand. Behind him Winston sits up and watches him in silence for a few moments.

WINSTON [*with a strange smile*]. You're counting!

JOHN [*with a start*]. What! Hey, Winston, you gave me a fright, man. I thought you were asleep. What's the matter? Can't you sleep?

WINSTON [*ignoring the question, still smiling*]. You've started counting the days now.

JOHN [*unable to resist the temptation to talk, moving over to Winston's bed*]. *Ja.*

WINSTON. How many?

JOHN. Ninety-two.

WINSTON. You see!

JOHN [*excited*]. Simple, man. Look . . . twenty days left in this month, thirty days in June, thirty-one in July, eleven days in August . . . ninety-two.

WINSTON [*still smiling, but watching John carefully*]. Tomorrow?

JOHN. Ninety-one.

WINSTON. And the next day?

JOHN. Ninety.

WINSTON. Then one day it will be eighty!

JOHN. *Ja!*

WINSTON. Then seventy.

JOHN. Hey, Winston, time doesn't pass so fast.

WINSTON. Then only sixty more days.

JOHN. That's just two months here on the Island.

WINSTON. Fifty . . . forty days in the quarry.

JOHN. Jesus, Winston!

WINSTON. Thirty.

JOHN. One month. Only one month to go.

WINSTON. Twenty . . . [*holding up his hands*] then ten . . . five, four, three, two . . . tomorrow!

[*The anticipation of that moment is too much for John.*]

JOHN. NO! Please, man, Winston. It hurts. Leave those three months alone. I'm going to sleep!

[*Back to his bed where he curls up in a tight ball and tries determinedly to sleep. Winston lies down again and stares up at the ceiling. After a pause he speaks quietly.*]

WINSTON. They won't keep you here for the full three months. Only two months. Then down to the jetty, into a ferry-boat . . . you'll say goodbye to this place . . . and straight to Victor Verster Prison on the mainland.

[*Against his will John starts to listen. He eventually sits upright and completely surrenders himself to Winston's description of the last few days of his confinement.*]

Life will change for you there. It will be much easier. Because you won't take Hodoshe with you. He'll stay here with me, on the Island. They'll put you to work in the vineyards at Victor Verster, John. There are no quarries there. Eating grapes, oranges . . . they'll change your diet . . . Diet C, and exercises so that you'll look good when they let you out finally. At night you'll play games . . . Ludo, draughts, snakes and ladders! Then one day they'll call you into the office, with a van waiting outside to take you back. The same five hundred miles. But this time they'll let you sit. You won't have to stand the whole way like you did coming here. And there won't be handcuffs. Maybe they'll even stop on the way so that you can have a pee. Yes, I'm sure they will. You might even sleep over somewhere. Then finally Port Elizabeth. Rooihel Prison again, John! That's very near home, man. New Brighton is next door! Through your cell window you'll see people moving up and down in the street, hear the buses roaring. Then one night you won't sleep again, because you'll be counting. Not days, as you are doing now, but hours. And the next morning, that beautiful morning, John,

they'll take you straight out of your cell to the Discharge
Office where they'll give you a new khaki shirt, long khaki
trousers, brown shoes. And your belongings! I almost forgot
your belongings.

JOHN. Hey, by the way! I was wearing a white shirt, black tie,
grey flannel trousers . . . brown Crockett shoes . . . socks? [*A
little laugh.*] I can't remember my socks! A check jacket . . . and
my watch! I was wearing my watch!

WINSTON. They'll wrap them up in a parcel. You'll have it
under your arm when they lead you to the gate. And outside,
John, outside that gate, New Brighton will be waiting for you.
Your mother, your father, Princess and the children . . . and
when they open it. . . .

[*Once again, but more violently this time, John breaks the mood as
the anticipation of the moment of freedom becomes too much for him.*]

JOHN. Stop it, Winston! Leave those three months alone for
Christ's sake. I want to sleep.

[*He tries to get away from Winston, but the latter goes after him.
Winston has now also abandoned his false smile.*]

WINSTON [*stopping John as he tries to crawl away*]. But it's not
finished, John!

JOHN. Leave me alone!

WINSTON. It doesn't end there. Your people will take you
home. Thirty-eight, Gratten Street, John! Remember it?
Everybody will be waiting for you . . . aunts, uncles, friends,
neighbours. They'll put you in a chair, John, like a king, give
you anything you want . . . cakes, sweets, cooldrinks . . . and
then you'll start to talk. You'll tell them about this place,
John, about Hodoshe, about the quarry, and about your good
friend Winston who you left behind. But you still won't be
happy, hey. Because you'll need a fuck. A really wild one!

JOHN. Stop it, Winston!

WINSTON [*relentless*]. And that is why at ten o'clock that
night you'll slip out through the back door and make your
way to Sky's place. Imagine it, man! All the boys waiting for
you . . . Georgie, Mangi, Vusumzi. They'll fill you up with
booze. They'll look after you. They know what it's like
inside. They'll fix you up with a woman. . . .

JOHN. NO!

WINSTON. Set you up with her in a comfortable joint, and then leave you alone. You'll watch her, watch her take her clothes off, you'll take your pants off, get near her, feel her, feel it. . . . Ja, you'll feel it. It will be wet. . . .

JOHN. WINSTON!

WINSTON. Wet *poes*, John! And you'll fuck it wild!

[*John turns finally to face Winston. A long silence as the two men confront each other. John is appalled at what he sees.*]

JOHN. Winston? What's happening? Why are you punishing me?

WINSTON [*quietly*]. You stink, John. You stink of beer, of company, of *poes*, of freedom. . . . Your freedom stinks, John, and it's driving me mad.

JOHN. No, Winston!

WINSTON. Yes! Don't deny it. Three months time, at this hour, you'll be wiping beer off your face, your hands on your balls, and *poes* waiting for you. You will laugh, you will drink, you will fuck and forget.

[*John's denials have no effect on Winston.*]

Stop bullshitting me! We've got no time left for that. There's only two months left between us. [*Pause.*] You know where I ended up this morning, John? In the quarry. Next to old Harry. Do you know old Harry, John?

JOHN. Yes.

WINSTON. Yes what? Speak, man!

JOHN. Old Harry, Cell Twenty-three, seventy years, serving Life!

WINSTON. That's not what I'm talking about. When you go to the quarry tomorrow, take a good look at old Harry. Look into his eyes, John. Look at his hands. They've changed him. They've turned him into stone. Watch him work with that chisel and hammer. Twenty perfect blocks of stone every day. Nobody else can do it like him. He loves stone. That's why they're nice to him. He's forgotten himself. He's forgotten everything . . . why he's here, where he comes from.
That's happening to me John. I've forgotten why I'm here.

JOHN. No.

WINSTON. Why am I here?

JOHN. You put your head on the block for others.

WINSTON. Fuck the others.

JOHN. Don't say that! Remember our ideals. . . .

WINSTON. Fuck our ideals. . . .

JOHN. No Winston . . . our slogans, our children's freedom. . . .

WINSTON. Fuck slogans, fuck politics . . . fuck everything, John. Why am I here? I'm jealous of your freedom, John. I also want to count. God also gave me ten fingers, but what do I count? My life? How do I count it, John? One . . . one . . . another day comes . . . one. . . . Help me, John! . . . Another day . . . one . . . one. . . . Help me, brother! . . . one. . . .

[*John has sunk to the floor, helpless in the face of the other man's torment and pain. Winston almost seems to bend under the weight of the life stretching ahead of him on the Island. For a few seconds he lives in silence with his reality, then slowly straightens up. He turns and looks at John. When he speaks again, it is the voice of a man who has come to terms with his fate, massively compassionate.*]

Nyana we Sizwe!

[*John looks up at him.*]

Nyana we Sizwe . . . it's all over now. All over. [*He moves over to John.*] Forget me. . . .

[*John attempts a last, limp denial.*]

No, John! Forget me . . . because I'm going to forget you. Yes, I will forget you. Others will come in here, John, count, go, and I'll forget them. Still more will come, count like you, go like you, and I will forget them. And then one day, it will all be over.

[*A lighting change suggests the passage of time. Winston collects together their props for Antigone.*]

Come. They're waiting.

JOHN. Do you know your words?

WINSTON. Yes. Come, we'll be late for the concert.

SCENE FOUR

The two men convert their cell-area into a stage for the prison concert. Their blankets are hung to provide a makeshift backdrop behind which Winston disappears with their props. John comes forward and addresses the audience. He is not yet in his Creon costume.

JOHN. Captain Prinsloo, Hodoshe, Warders, . . . and Gentlemen! Two brothers of the House of Labdacus found themselves on opposite sides in battle, the one defending the State, the other attacking it. They both died on the battlefield. King Creon, Head of the State, decided that the one who had defended the State would be buried with all religious rites due to the noble dead. But the other one, the traitor Polynices, who had come back from exile intending to burn and destroy his fatherland, to drink the blood of his masters, was to have no grave, no mourning. He was to lie on the open fields to rot, or at most be food for the jackals. It was a law. But Antigone, their sister, defied the law and buried the body of her brother Polynices. She was caught and arrested. That is why tonight the Hodoshe Span, Cell Forty-two, presents for your entertainment: 'The Trial and Punishment of Antigone'.

[He disappears behind the blankets. They simulate a fanfare of trumpets. At its height the blankets open and he steps out as Creon. In addition to his pendant, there is some sort of crown and a blanket draped over his shoulders as a robe.]

My People! Creon stands before his palace and greets you! Stop! Stop! What's that I hear? You, good man, speak up. Did I hear 'Hail the King'? My good people, I am your *servant* . . . a happy one, but still your servant. How many times must I ask you, implore you to see in these symbols of office nothing more, or less, than you would in the uniform of the humblest menial in your house. Creon's crown is as simple, and I hope as clean, as the apron Nanny wears. And even as Nanny smiles and is your happy servant because she sees her charge . . . your child! . . . waxing fat in that little cradle, so too does Creon—your obedient servant!—stand here and smile. For what does he see? Fatness and happiness! How else does one measure the success of a state? By the sumptuousness of the palaces built for its king and princes? The magnificence of the temples erected to its gods? The achievements of its scientists and technicians who can now send rockets to the moon? No! These count for nothing beside the fatness and happiness of its people.

But have you ever paused to ask yourself whose responsibility it is to maintain that fatness and happiness? The answer is simple, is it not? . . . your servant the king! But have you then gone on to ask yourself what does the king need to maintain this happy state of affairs? What, other than his silly crown, are the tools with which a king fashions the happiness of his people? The answer is equally simple, my good people. The law! Yes. The law. A three-lettered word, and how many times haven't you glibly used it, never bothering to ask yourselves, 'What then is the law?' Or if you have, then making recourse to such clichés as 'the law states this . . . or the law states that'. The law states or maintains nothing, good people. The law defends! The law is no more or less than a shield in your faithful servant's hand to protect YOU! But even as a shield would be useless in one hand, to defend, without a sword in the other, to strike . . . so too the law has its edge. The penalty! We have come through difficult times. I am sure it is needless for me to remind you of the constant troubles on our borders . . . those despicable rats who would gnaw away at our fatness and happiness. We have been diligent in dealing with them. But unfortunately there are still at large subversive elements . . . there are still amongst us a few rats that are not satisfied and to them I must show this face of Creon . . . so different to the one that hails my happy people! It is with a heavy heart, and you shall see why soon enough, that I must tell you that we have caught another one. That is why I have assembled you here. Let what follows be a living lesson for those among you misguided enough still to harbour sympathy for rats! The shield has defended. Now the sword must strike!

Bring in the accused.

[*Winston, dressed as Antigone, enters. He wears the wig, the necklace of nails, and a blanket around his waist as a skirt.*]

Your name!

WINSTON. Antigone, daughter of Oedipus, sister of Eteocles and Polynices.

JOHN. You are accused that, in defiance of the law, you buried the body of the traitor Polynices.

WINSTON. I buried the body of my brother Polynices.

JOHN. Did you know there was a law forbidding that?

WINSTON. Yes.

JOHN. Yet you defied it.

WINSTON. Yes.

JOHN. Did you know the consequences of such defiance?

WINSTON. Yes.

JOHN. What did you plead to the charges laid against you? Guilty or Not Guilty?

WINSTON. Guilty.

JOHN. Antigone, you have pleaded guilty. Is there anything you wish to say in mitigation? This is your last chance. Speak.

WINSTON. Who made the law forbidding the burial of my brother?

JOHN. The State.

WINSTON. Who is the State?

JOHN. As King I am its manifest symbol

WINSTON. So you made the law.

JOHN. Yes, for the State.

WINSTON. Are you God?

JOHN. Watch your words, little girl!

WINSTON. You said it was my chance to speak.

JOHN. But not to ridicule.

WINSTON. I've got no time to waste on that. Your sentence on my life hangs waiting on your lips.

JOHN. Then speak on.

WINSTON. When Polynices died in battle, all that remained was the empty husk of his body. He could neither harm nor help any man again. What lay on the battlefield waiting for Hodoshe to turn rotten, belonged to God. You are only a man, Creon. Even as there are laws made by men, so too there are others that come from God. He watches my soul for a transgression even as your spies hide in the bush at night to see who is transgressing your laws. Guilty against God I will not be for any man on this earth. Even without your law, Creon, and the threat of death to whoever defied it, I know I must die. Because of your law and my defiance, that fate is now very near. So much the better. Your threat is nothing to me, Creon. But if I had let my mother's son, a Son of the Land, lie there as food for the carrion fly, Hodoshe, my soul would never have known peace. Do you understand anything of what I am saying, Creon?

JOHN. Your words reveal only that obstinacy of spirit which has brought nothing but tragedy to your people. First you break the law. Now you insult the State.

WINSTON. Just because I ask you to remember that you are only a man?

JOHN. And to add insult to injury you gloat over your deeds! No, Antigone, you will not escape with impunity. Were you my own child you would not escape full punishment.

WINSTON. Full punishment? Would you like to do more than just kill me?

JOHN. That is all I wish.

WINSTON. Then let us not waste any time. Stop talking. I buried my brother. That is an honourable thing, Creon. All these people in your state would say so too, if fear of you and another law did not force them into silence.

JOHN. You are wrong. None of my people think the way you do.

WINSTON. Yes they do, but no one dares tell you so. You will not sleep peacefully, Creon.

JOHN. You add shamelessness to your crimes, Antigone.

WINSTON. I do not feel any shame at having honoured my brother.

JOHN. Was he that died with him not also your brother?

WINSTON. He was.

JOHN. And so you honour the one and insult the other.

WINSTON. I shared my love, not my hate.

JOHN. Go then and share your love among the dead. I will have no rats' law here while yet I live.

WINSTON. We are wasting time, Creon. Stop talking. Your words defeat your purpose. They are prolonging my life.

JOHN [*again addressing the audience*]. You have heard all the relevant facts. Needless now to call the state witnesses who would testify beyond reasonable doubt that the accused is guilty. Nor, for that matter, is it in the best interests of the State to disclose their identity. There was a law. The law was broken. The law stipulated its penalty. My hands are tied.

Take her from where she stands, straight to the Island! There wall her up in a cell for life, with enough food to acquit ourselves of the taint of her blood.

WINSTON [*to the audience*]. Brothers and Sisters of the Land! I go now on my last journey. I must leave the light of day forever, for the Island, strange and cold, to be lost between life and death. So, to my grave, my everlasting prison, condemned alive to solitary death.

[*Tearing off his wig and confronting the audience as Winston, not Antigone.*]

Gods of our Fathers! My Land! My Home!

Time waits no longer. I go now to my living death, because I honoured those things to which honour belongs.

[*The two men take off their costumes and then strike their 'set'. They then come together and, as in the beginning, their hands come together to suggest handcuffs, and their right and left legs to suggest ankle-chains. They start running . . . John mumbling a prayer, and Winston a rhythm for their three-legged run.*
The siren wails.
Fade to blackout.]

STATEMENTS
AFTER AN ARREST UNDER
THE IMMORALITY ACT

by
ATHOL FUGARD

CHARACTERS

A WHITE WOMAN (Frieda Joubert)
A COLOURED MAN (Errol Philander)
A POLICEMAN (Detective-Sergeant J. du Preez)

This play was given its first performance on 22 January 1974 at the Royal Court Theatre, London, and was directed by Athol Fugard with the following cast:

Frieda Joubert	Yvonne Bryceland
Errol Philander	Ben Kingsley
Detective-Sergeant J. du Preez	Wilson Dunster

STATEMENTS AFTER AN ARREST UNDER
THE IMMORALITY ACT

A man *and* a woman *on a blanket on the floor. Both of them are naked. He is caressing her hair.*
Dim light.

WOMAN [*shyly*]. I dried it in the sun. Just sat there, on a chair in the backyard, feeling the warmth of it on my head. Every strand felt separate and my head very light.... The texture of the hair changes as it dries. And then the smell of it when it falls over my face... the smell of clean hair and shampoo. The warmer it gets the more you smell it. And if there's a breeze, even a small one, the way it lifts and floats. Also... the colour of the strands, specially when they hang close to your eyes.... The colour seems to pulse. [*Pause.*] There's no sense of time. Everything very still. Just the sounds of a warm afternoon... warm sounds, warm smells... specially the fig tree. A lot of the fruit has fallen now and burst, rotting on the ground... almost like wine! The leaves also have a very strong smell when it's hot. [*Pause.*] What else?... Doves... a locust flying suddenly... bees... Just sat there.... Quiet Saturday afternoon... hearing and smelling it all quietly, being very lazy and thinking all sorts of things.

[*Turning to the man.*]

And you?

MAN. Oh... another day. Nothing special... until now.

WOMAN. I don't care. Tell me.

MAN. There's nothing to tell. I did a bit of work at the school.... No! Of course! I know what happened today.

WOMAN. Tell me.

MAN. I built a five-roomed house. [*She laughs.*] I did! Lunch-time. On the way home I passed a little boy... Izak... his older brother Henry started school this year... Izak Tobias... anyway Izak was playing there in the sand with some old bricks and things. I stopped and watched him. Building himself a house he said. Told me all about it. His mother and his father and his baby brother sleep in one room, and he and his sister and his granny in the other. Two rooms. It's the house he lives in. I know. I've been in it. It's a Bontrug house. [*Pause.*] You know what I made him do? Build a separate room for his granny. Then I explained that when his sister got big she would need a room for herself. So he built another one for her. When I left him he had a five-roomed house and a garage. . . . That's what it's all about, hey.

WOMAN. Yes.

MAN. If you're going to dream, give yourself five rooms, man.

[*Silence.*]

WOMAN. I love you. [*Pause.*] What's the matter? What are you doing?

[*A match flares in the darkness. She scrambles away.*]

WOMAN. No!

MAN. Please.

WOMAN. No!!

[*The match dies. Darkness.*]

MAN. Is it me or you?

WOMAN. You don't understand.

MAN. Understand what? There is seeing, and being seen. Which one are you frightened of? Me or you?

WOMAN. It's not as simple as that!

MAN. Yes, it is! It's got to be . . . sometimes.

That last book you lent me ends off a chapter with a paragraph, and the paragraph ends off his speculation about the origin of life . . . conclusions . . . vague. Nobody will ever know. . . . 'These questions cannot be answered at this point and are perhaps unanswerable.' But we do know that the difference between life and even the most complex of chemical processes are four-fold . . . metabolic processes of a wide but not unlimited variety; a degree of independence from the environment; sexual reproduction; and, finally, a susceptibility to death. Because life lives, life must die. Simple. [*Pause.*] Moon's nearly full out there tonight you know. Toringberg will be splendid when I walk back. Hell, Frieda, if we could have opened those curtains . . . !

WOMAN. Don't! Please. . . .

MAN. Why? What about me? I want to be seen. I want you to see me. [*Moves suddenly into a faint patch of light from the curtained window.*] The brightest spot in our world. Here I am. Me. Can you see me?

WOMAN. Yes.

MAN. And?

WOMAN. I see you.

MAN. Frieda! Frieda! Life . . . is three billion years old. Fact. This little piece of the earth, the few miserable square feet of this room . . . this stupid little town, this desert . . . was a sea, millions and millions of years ago. Dinosaurs wallowed here! Truly. That last book mentions us: 'The richest deposits . . . Permian and Triassic periods . . . are to be found in the Graaff Reinet district of the Cape Province of South Africa.' Us. Our world. Are you listening?

WOMAN. Yes.

MAN. You *can* see me?

WOMAN. Yes.

MAN. You want to hear more?

WOMAN. Yes.

MAN [*thinks . . . then*]. There was a point . . . a billion or so years after the beginning of the earth, when the surface cooled sufficiently to permit water to accumulate in liquid form. Up until then it had just been gaseous, remember. But when this stage was reached . . . [*Pause.*] It rained continuously for millions of years.

Rain . . . water . . . on and on. . . . [*Pause.*] Frieda? [*Holds out his hand. She moves to him, but remains shy and reticent.*] What are you frightened of?

WOMAN. Everything. Me . . . you . . . them. . . .

MAN. Them?

WOMAN. No. That as well of course. But I wasn't thinking about them now. [*Pause.*] The dinosaurs and those hairy . . . missing links . . . that look like baboons, stand like men, and could almost smile.

MAN. Australopithecus. Fossilized skull in a limestone quarry in Taung, Bechuanaland. Raymond Dart. 1930.

WOMAN. Is that the one . . . ?

MAN. Yes. That's the one you don't like.

WOMAN. With the females and their babies . . . looking so. . . .

MAN. Yes. [*Laughing.*] You're frightened of him! You know who I am frightened of? Bishop Ussher. God created the world . . . the act of creation took place on October the twenty-sixth, four thousand and four B.C., at nine a.m.

WOMAN. You shouldn't. . . .

MAN. He worked it out. From the Bible. [*Pause.*] Come.

WOMAN. Try . . . please try to understand.

MAN. No. You understand. Do you think I just want to *see* you? Do you think I just want to look? [*Pause.*] I do. [*Pause.*] Listen to this one: ' . . . no vestige of a beginning and no prospect of an end . . .'. Did you hear that?

WOMAN. Yes.

MAN. And? Listen again. ' . . . no vestige of a beginning and no prospect of an end'. The conclusion of Charles Lyell after a good look at what was happening on the surface of the earth. *Principles of Geology*, 1830. What does that do to you?

WOMAN. Nothing.

[*Pause. He laughs quietly.*]

MAN. You're wrong. You're so wrong. If it wasn't for that sentence . . . I don't think we should have ever met. Hey, when did . . . ?

WOMAN. Almost a year ago. January the twenty-sixth.

MAN. Then it was the night of January the twenty-fifth. My family were already asleep. It was quiet . . . the best time to read or study. . . . The lamp on the table, me, one of Bontrug's mongrels barking outside in the dark. . . . Anyway, I was reading, understanding everything clearly . . . fact after fact . . . the time it all took. . . . So slow . . . God is so lazy, Frieda! . . . and then suddenly those words: ' . . . no vestige of a beginning, no prospect of an end. . . .' I stopped. I had to. I couldn't go further. They weren't just words, it wasn't just that I understood that somebody had said . . . I'm expressing myself badly. It's hard to describe. It was almost like having a . . . No! . . . it was a 'comprehension'—*ja*, of life and time . . . and there in the middle of it . . . at that precise moment . . . in Bontrug, was me. Being me, just being me there in that little room was . . . [*choosing his words carefully*] . . .

the most exciting thing that had ever happened to me. I wanted that moment to last forever! It was so intense it almost hurt. I couldn't sit still.

I just left the book . . . didn't look at it again . . . I didn't want to see another word, read another fact. . . . *Ja!* It wasn't a question of facts any more, something else, something bigger. I went outside. Walking round Bontrug. I looked at the Bontrug *braks* with their tails between their legs. . . . Dogs. . . . I stopped in front of old Tobias' little place with the five of them inside at that moment sleeping on the floor. . . . I looked at it and said 'House' . . . at the stars. . . . My hands were cold . . . but ten fingers, Frieda. . . . If I was the first man I could have started to count the stars.

There was nothing I was frightened to see.

WOMAN. You've never told me about that before.
[*Pause.*]

MAN [*as if he hadn't heard her*]. So, the next morning there I was on . . . what did you say it was . . . the twenty-sixth . . . January the twenty-sixth . . . asking if you had

WOMAN. Julian Huxley's *Principles of Evolution*. [*Pause.*] Why . . . why have you waited, almost a year . . . to tell me about that?

MAN. I've told no one.

WOMAN. I'm not no one. I'm also me. I'm the other person on the floor. With you. [*Pause.*] I'm jealous. You can make me so jealous. And I'm frightened. Yes. And there are things I don't want to see. . . . They found two snakes in my neighbour's backyard yesterday . . . Mr. van Wyk. . . .

MAN. What were they?

WOMAN. Somebody said they were rinkhals.

MAN. Rinkhals, the drought's bringing them out. We've had no trouble in Bontrug.

WOMAN. They killed them.

MAN. Well, if they were rinkhals . . . old people say, if they sit up in your footpath, they can spit you blind.

WOMAN. Mr. van Wyk . . . said they were mating at the time. Their . . . the pieces kept moving . . . for a long time afterwards.

MAN. *Ja* . . . it's the nervous system. . . . I think they die later or something.

[*Pause. He feels around in the darkness for his trousers.*]
What's the time?

WOMAN. No . . . not yet. I'm sorry. Please. Say it again.

MAN. What?

WOMAN. Those words . . . that sentence. . . .

MAN. ' . . . no vestige of a beginning and no prospect of an end.'

WOMAN. Did it work?

MAN. *Ja.*

WOMAN. Good. [*She draws closer to him out of the darkness*]. It's so quiet. Just those dogs.

[*Pause. He listens.*]

MAN. Town dogs.

WOMAN. What makes you so sure?

MAN. I've walked past them.

[*He has removed a few coins from his trouser pocket and is idly trying to count them in the dark.*]
Which ones have got the ridges round them?

WOMAN. What?

MAN. Coins. Which ones have got those little ridges?

WOMAN. Two cents and one cent.

MAN [*counting*]. Five . . . seven . . . seventeen.

WOMAN. About two years ago I thought of leaving here. Going back to Cradock.

MAN. Why didn't you?

WOMAN. Too much bother I suppose.

MAN. What was it like?

WOMAN. Cradock?

MAN. Yes.

WOMAN. You've been there.

MAN. I mean . . . were you happy there?

WOMAN [*after a pause*]. My first memory is being very small and sitting on the floor of the long passageway in our house. The shutters must have been closed because it was all dark and quiet. Then somebody opened the front door at the other end and suddenly I saw all the sunlight and noise of the street outside. I started to walk towards it, but before I could get there the door closed. I was so upset! I sat down and cried and cried. [*Pause.*] My last memory of Cradock is locking that same door from the outside, and taking the keys to the estate agent.

MAN. You sold the house.

WOMAN. Yes . . . after my mother died, and I got the job here.

MAN. What else?

WOMAN. That's all.

MAN [*the coins in his hand*]. Forty-three.

WOMAN. What?

MAN. Forty-three cents.

WOMAN. Are you sure you are happy?

MAN. Of course. It was good, man. Wasn't it?

WOMAN. Yes.

MAN. Do you ever do that? Imagine that what you've got in your pockets is all you've got, but really all you've got. No family, no place to go, nothing to do, just standing suddenly in Church Street with forty-three cents . . . and then try to work out what you would do with it.

WOMAN. No.

MAN. Ten cents for bread . . . that would last the whole day . . . ten cents for cooldrink.

WOMAN. Buy milk.

MAN. No. When we're thirsty we drink cooldrink. Twenty-three cents left. What would you do? What do you think you'd want? You got something to eat, you're not thirsty.

WOMAN. Save something for tomorrow.

MAN. No. There's no tomorrow. Just today.

WOMAN. Why not?

MAN. Just part of the game.

WOMAN. I don't like the game.

MAN [*in vacant fascination with the thought of himself, one day, and twenty-three cents*].

Could buy a newspaper. Read what happened in the world

yesterday. Seventeen cents left. Place like Cape Town that could be bus fare. Go and look at the sea. Here you could only spend it in the shops.

Buy a stamp, post a letter!

WOMAN. Envelope and writing-paper?

MAN. That's true.

Could you send a telegram for twenty-three cents?

WOMAN. If the address and message was short enough.

MAN. How short?

WOMAN. I don't know.

MAN. Let's say ten words. [*Counting them on his fingers.*] 'Give us this day our daily bread.' Three left for my name and His address. What's your message?

WOMAN. 'Forgive us our trespasses as we forgive those who. . . .'

MAN. You haven't even got enough for the message! I still haven't spent the twenty-three cents. Shops close at six. *Ja!* That's what would do it. Twenty-three cents and the shops closing. That's how I'd make my mistake. I'd be too late for anything except twenty-three cents of sweets, or six stale cakes. Eat them all and be sick. What would you do?

WOMAN. Am I alone?

MAN. What do you mean?

WOMAN. Do I have you?

MAN. No. I haven't got you. You haven't got me. All you've got is forty-three cents, and one day. [*Feels for her hand in the dark and gives her the money.*] What would you do with it?

WOMAN. Nothing.

MAN. Nothing! You wouldn't. . . .

WOMAN. No, I wouldn't. I wouldn't even have bought bread. [*Pause.*]

MAN. The only reason I bought it was because. . . .

WOMAN. You had nothing except forty-three cents and one day.

MAN. *Ja.* I'm a *brak*, hey!

WOMAN. No.

MAN. It's true. I'm hungry enough to make every mistake . . .

88

even bark. [*Pause.*] But if that one day also had a real chance to start again—you know, to make everything different—and forty-three cents would buy me even just the first brick for a five-roomed house . . . I'd spend it on that and go hungry. [*Pause.*] Anyway listen. I'm going to try hard now to look after things. Okay? Give me one more chance, man.

WOMAN. Don't ask for that. You are my chance. I don't want to lose it.

MAN. It all goes wrong because I don't! Like my correspondence course. Three assignments unopened. In my drawer. Twenty-five rand. That's no good. I must finish it. I've got all the time until school starts. And this year . . . I'm really going to teach. You watch.

And stop hurting you. I don't do it on purpose. I don't want to hurt you. I love you. But hell, it's just so useless at times I can't help it. And then that makes me feel even worse. Some of those walks back have been hard. Specially when I wanted to turn round and come back and say I'm sorry but you know you can't.

[*Pause.*]

Hey. You know what I was thinking coming here? I must try and buy a car this year. Good second-hand car.

[*A sudden noise startles them. They scramble apart, the woman grabbing the blanket and covering herself.*]

Ssssh!! [*Pause.*] Sure you locked it?

WOMAN [*nodding*]. Back door?

MAN. Yes. [*Tense, motionless pause as they listen in silence for a few seconds longer. The man moves to his clothes on the floor.*] Hot tonight, hey.

WOMAN. Do you want the towel?

MAN. *Ja*, okay. I'm sweating. [*The woman finds a towel, takes it to him.*] There's no water left in Bontrug.

WOMAN. We're going to have prayers for rain next week. Wednesday.

MAN. The location dam is empty. Little mud left for the goats. They're going to start bringing in for us on Monday. Got to be ready with our buckets at twelve. Two for each house.

WOMAN. Then why won't you let me send you some of mine?

The borehole is still very strong. Please! It would be so easy.

MAN. Thanks, but I'll go along with Bontrug.

WOMAN. Don't thank me for something you won't take.

MAN. For the thought then.

WOMAN. To hell with the thought! I'm not trying to be kind. It's only water, and you need it.

MAN. We all do.

WOMAN. Exactly! So your family must suffer because of your pride.

MAN [disbelief]. Pride?

WOMAN. It sounds like it.

MAN. Pride doesn't use back doors!

WOMAN. Sssh, please!

MAN. Or wait until it's dark. You don't walk the way I do between the location and town with pride.

WOMAN. Please don't let's argue tonight.

MAN. Okay. [Defeated by her apparent lack of understanding, he turns away from her to his clothes. For a few seconds he tries to sort them out, then stops. He confronts her again.] Water. Water, man. You know . . . water!

I wanted to wash before I came here tonight.

Your water. You want to send me some of your water. Is it so hard to understand? Because if you can't . . . ! Why do you think it's easy? Is that what I look like? Is that why they're so nice to me out there? Because I'm easy? But when for once I get so . . . I feel so buggered-up inside that I say 'No' instead of 'Yes' . . . I'm proud! Proud! I teach children how to spell that word. I say to them: 'Proud as a Peacock!' Me? Holding my breath and sweating, really sweating, man, because suddenly we heard something and I thought: 'They've found us! Run!' Coming here tonight I heard a car coming, from the location. . . . I hid under that little bridge over the spruit . . . people relieve themselves there! . . . I was on my hands and knees among the shit, waiting for that car to pass, so that Bontrug won't start asking, 'Why is the Meester walking into town every night?' [Stopping her from moving away.] No! Please listen. I must talk. When I take that same walk just now . . . back . . . out there in the dark where the tar and the light ends, where the stones start. I'm going to sit down and say to myself: 'Back home again!' . . . and hate it. *Ja*. Hate it! Bontrug. The *braks* that run out at me when I get there. My school. The children I teach. My home. The same world I looked at that night a year ago and said 'Mine!!' and was excited that I was there, in it! Easy to hate, man, when you suddenly find you're always walking back to it . . . and I am. Whatever happens I'm going to be there walking back to it. So I say to myself: 'Careful, Philander. It's yours. It's all you can ever really have. Love it. You've got to.' Sometimes that's easy too. But you see, even when I do . . . there's still you. I'm in the shit, hey. That's how I walk now between Bontrug and the town . . . one way guilty, back with. . . . [*Pause.*] I'll tell you something else. Coming here once . . . in the 'old' days . . . I passed a man and a woman and their child . . . little boy . . . going back to the location. They got names, but it doesn't matter. You don't know them. They had stopped half-way up the hill to rest. It's hard walking up there with the sun on your back. All three of them . . . hot and unwashed. They smell. Because I was coming to you, you know what I saw? Rags. I don't mean their clothes. The people inside looked like rags. The man drinks too much, he's a useless rag. The woman's an old rag. Their child is going to be somebody's good rag, until. . . . What do you do with yours? I was looking at my feet when I walked past them. Frieda! . . . [*shaking his head*] . . . when I realized that . . . when I realized what I . . . I wanted to call them and bring them with me to the library. I wanted to knock on that back door and stand there with them when you opened it. I wanted you to see me with them! What would you have done? Asked them in? Called them Miester and Miesies? Would you have given them tea in your cups? How long before you would have started waiting for them to go? You understand now. The reason I don't want your water is just because Bontrug is thirsty.

WOMAN. And that is not pride.

MAN. No. Exactly the opposite. Shame.

WOMAN. I don't understand . . . anything.

MAN. Then you can't. Don't even try. [*He turns away from her back to his clothes and puts on his vest.*]

WOMAN. It really would be better if you could wait until it's darker. [*He stops. Pause.*] Old Mrs. Buys is still staring and being strange. She changed her books again today. I might be wrong but. . . . She's taken out more books this month than she did the whole of last year.

MAN. And you think I'm proud.

WOMAN. You should be . . . of some things. [*Pause.*] I didn't think you were going to come.

MAN. I couldn't help myself.

WOMAN. Didn't you want to?

MAN. No, I wanted to. But I thought maybe you'd had enough of me for a while. . . .

WOMAN. That's not true.

MAN. I haven't been cheerful company lately.

[*Pause.*]

WOMAN. What must I do? Please tell me.

MAN. Don't say that.

WOMAN. I've got to. What will make you happy?

MAN. Something that doesn't hurt anybody.

WOMAN. We do?

MAN. Yes.

WOMAN. Your family?

MAN. Not we. I do.

WOMAN. It's the holiday, isn't it?

MAN. That's one thing.

WOMAN. Listen. Stop worrying about it. Take your family. I promise I'll understand.
We won't talk about it again.

MAN. I don't want to go. I decided to settle it last night after supper. Be firm with them, I said to myself. Explain you need the time for the course. Before I could bring up the subject, they started talking. When must they start packing? How much they were looking forward to it! Selina hasn't seen her mother for three years. I couldn't even open my mouth. I'm so bloody sick of my lies.

WOMAN. How much do you think your wife . . . ?

MAN. I don't know. I can't tell. I can't see or do anything properly any more, except come here, and even that I do thinking it's a mistake. [*Pause.*] No, she knows nothing. How can she? She doesn't have tea with your old Mrs. Buys. She thinks I'm tired! Been studying too hard. All I need is a good holiday. Jesus, they're so innocent.

WOMAN. Even if you could, you would never leave them.

MAN. I don't know.

WOMAN. No! Tell the truth, please.
Even if you could you would never leave them.

[*Pause.*]

MAN. No. I would never leave them. I'm not . . . strong enough to hurt them, for something I wanted.
What would happen to them if I did?

WOMAN. Go home. Take your conscience and your guilt and go back to Bontrug and look after your family. I've also got problems. I can't add your adultery to them. If you haven't got the courage to say No . . . to anybody . . . me or her . . . I'll do it for you. Go home.

MAN [*viciously*]. It would be better if I waited until it's dark . . . remember! [*Pause.*] My adultery? And yours? *Ja.* Yours! If that's true of me because of you and my wife, then just as much for you because of me and your white skin. Maybe you are married to that they way I am to Bontrug.
You sneak out of it the way I sneak out of my house to come here. Let me see you choose!!

WOMAN. I will. Take me with you. Now.

[*Silence.*]

MAN. You're right. I'm a coward.

WOMAN. Is there nothing we can do any more except hurt each other?

MAN. One day when I was a boy, my father came home after work to our hut on the farm. He brought with him a jackal's foot. The animal had escaped that way . . . chewed off the foot caught in the trap. For a long time I waited for the story of the dogs that had caught and killed a jackal with only three legs. You see, I could only think about how much it must have hurt to do that. I didn't know anything yet about being so frightened of something else, that you would do that to yourself. [*Pause.*] That's what we're doing . . . chewing away, chewing away. And if we're frightened enough . . . we'll escape . . . but. . . . [*Pause.*] What's the time?

WOMAN. Too dark. I can't see the clock. Or you.

MAN. I'm here.

WOMAN. What are you doing?

MAN. Nothing.
And you?

WOMAN. Waiting. . . .

[*Pause.*]

MAN. For what?

WOMAN. I don't know. I suppose the dogs.

MAN. Frieda. [*Holding out a hand in the dark.*] Frieda!

[*A moment's hesitation and then they impulsively come together and embrace. Against this image of the two lovers,* a plain-clothes police-man, Detective Sergeant J. du Preez, *walks on. He carries a police dossier and notebook. His statement is dictated to the audience.*]

POLICEMAN. Frieda Joubert. Ten, Conradie Street. European.
Errol Philander. Bontrug Location. Coloured.
Charge: Immorality Act.
Joubert runs the library in the town. Been living here for six years. Unmarried. No previous convictions.
Errol Philander is Principal of the location school. Born here. Wife and one child. No previous convictions.
My suspicions were first aroused by a report from Mrs. Tienie Buys.

[*Abandoning 'dictation' . . . he takes a statement out of the police dossier and reads it aloud.*]

Statement to Detective Sergeant J. du Preez at the Noupoort Police Station on December the seventeenth: 'My attention was first drawn to the behaviour of Joubert and Philander on a night in June last year. Late that afternoon I was down at the bottom of my garden when I saw Philander arrive at the back door of the library and without knocking, go in. A few moments later, the light in the back room of the library was put on. Some time later Joubert herself came out and emptied some rubbish in the dirt bin. At about eight o'clock that night I was down at the bottom of my garden again and I noticed that the light was still on. I'd no sooner noticed this when it was switched off. No other lights were on in the library. I waited to see what would happen next. After some time—about forty-five minutes of darkness—the back door opened and Philander came out.

He closed the door behind him, locked it with a key which he put in his trouser pocket, and walked away. This pattern of events—Philander's arrival followed by a period of darkness until he left—was repeated on many occasions between that night and today . . . December the seventeenth. I also noticed that his movements became more and more secretive over the six months. I am prepared to repeat this statement under oath in Court.

Signed: Mrs. Tienie Buys, 2 Riebeeck Street, Noupoort.'

[*Replaces the statement in the dossier. He continues his 'dictation' to the audience.*]

Mrs. Buys's back garden is immediately behind the library. On her side there is a row of quince trees. The back entrance to the library—which leads directly into the room Joubert uses as an office, and in which the two of them were arrested tonight—can be clearly seen from under these trees. I asked Mrs. Buys to contact me the next time Philander arrived at the library. She did this the very next afternoon, the twenty-ninth. I watched the library back entrance from under the trees at the bottom of Mrs. Buys's garden. After at least an hour of darkness, Philander came out of the back door, locked it behind him, put the key in his pocket, and walked away. I went round quickly to the corner of Church and Conradie Streets. I was just in time to see Joubert leaving by the front door. I decided that these events warranted a thorough investigation of the whole matter. The library was kept under observation. Philander visited it every day. On a further three occasions the pattern of events was suspicious. After discussion with Warrant Officer Pieterse it was decided that Joubert and Philander should be apprehended at the next opportunity. It was also decided that a camera should be used to obtain photographic evidence of the suspected offence. On the twelfth of January, Constable Harvey, who had been keeping a watch on the library reported in the late afternoon that Philander had arrived and was in the building with Joubert. Together with Harvey and Sergeant Smit, we went to Mrs. Buys's back garden. We waited from six o'clock to eight o'clock. Constable Harvey reported that nobody had left through the front door. We climbed over the fence, and in the dark made our way to the back door. Even though it and the window was closed, we could clearly hear voices whispering inside. On a sign from me the window was forced open, and a torch shone into the room. I saw Joubert and Philander lying side by side on a blanket on the floor. She was naked and he appeared to be wearing a vest. Sergeant Smit started to take photographs.

[*A blackout, during which the policeman exits. A sequence of camera flashes in the darkness exposes the man and the woman tearing apart from their embrace; the man then scrambling for his trousers, finding them, and trying to put them on; the woman, naked, crawling around on the floor, looking for the man. As she finds him, and tries to hide behind his back, the flashes stop and torches are shone on them. The woman scrambles away, finds the blanket, and covers herself. The torches are relentless, but we never see anything of the men behind them. These 'flash-sequences' are nightmare excursions into the split second of exposure and must be approached as 'sub-text' rather than 'reality'.*]

MAN [*terrified. Covering his genitals with his trousers he talks desperately to the torch shining on him.*] Look . . . look—before you make up your mind let me tell you something. . . . I'm . . . I'm Principal. . . . I . . . I won't do it again. . . . I'm frightened. *Ja*, I'm frightened.

[*Blinking back at the torch with terror he tries to get into his trousers without exposing himself. He can't manage it. The operation becomes a nightmare. For a few seconds the woman watches him with vacant horror. Then she scrambles forward and, using her blanket, tries to shield him while she talks compulsively to the torches. Her first words are an almost incoherent babble. As she moves around, the torches follow her. Finding himself in darkness, the man gets slowly to his feet, retrieves his hat, and then tries— carefully and quietly—to get away.*]

WOMAN. Tennis biscuits! Only one. In the afternoons I have

my tea at four. I like to make it myself. The tea things are kept in my office, nice and neat on a tray under a clean drying-up cloth. I can see the library clock from my desk. I was . . . [*Pause.*] I was waiting for him. I was always waiting for him. I tried as long as I could to think he might still come. Then at half-past five I thought to myself . . . No, he's not going to . . . and suddenly . . . nothing. There was . . . nothing. Just lock up and go home, have supper, go to bed, try to sleep so that tomorrow and its chance of seeing him would come.

I locked the library door—I was hating myself for having waited—walked back into the office, and there he was. He looked tired, hot, his shoes were dusty. We talked a bit. But I didn't really listen to him because . . . he wasn't really talking to me. I could see something was wrong, that he was still unhappy, so I went to the desk—I was carrying a pile of books. . . . The new books have come! . . .

I was trying to work out what I could expect. I knew he was going to hurt me . . . I mean, not on purpose, but it just seems we can't avoid it. So I waited for it. It came. He said he supposed he shouldn't have come.

[*Pause.*]

I didn't want to stay there then, in the office I mean, so I took the books I had sorted out and went into the library. But I didn't want to be there either! I had to go back because I couldn't leave it like that. When I did he said he was sorry and that he hadn't meant it. I was at the desk again stamping books and just wishing he would stop saying and doing all the things that always made him feel so sorry! It was getting dark and I had that hopeless feeling inside. He tried to explain, again. Said it was because of the way he was neglecting things —me, his family, his correspondence course, his school—all the things that really mattered in his life because they all still did, only he felt he'd become so useless at looking after them. I told him . . . I said, he wasn't neglecting me and that even if he did I would understand so he shouldn't worry about it, but he said he did, because he loved us all—me, his family, his school. . . . [*Pause.*] I was feeling terribly lonely again. We seemed so far away from each other and I didn't know why, or what to do. It was dark. I couldn't see properly where to stamp the books any more. I should have put on the light.

But I just went on stamping and wishing it would get still darker so that everything would disappear—him, me, the room, what I was feeling—just disappear. . . . [*Frightened of what she had just said; very loudly . . .*] No. No!

[*One of the torches leaves her abruptly and picks up the man still trying to get away. He drops his trousers with fright and shields his genitals with his hat. He listens carefully to what the woman is saying.*]

He stopped talking suddenly, and stood up. I had given him a fright. He asked me what was wrong. I just said . . . 'Nothing.' We were whispering. Whispering makes you sweat. He loosened his tie and said. . . .

[*The man realizes he must stop, and correct, this vein of intimate confession. With a sign to the torch he puts his hat on, then steps forward and faces her, and then takes his hat off in the correct and respectful manner.*]

MAN. Miss Frieda Joubert?

[*The woman stops talking, turns, and looks at him. She can't believe what she sees. She laughs with bewildered innocence. The man accepts her amusement. He handles his hat with a suggestion of nervousness as he starts to talk, respectfully.*]

There's no water left in Bontrug. The dam's empty. Little mud left for the goats. They're going to start bringing in for us on Monday. We've been told to be ready with our buckets at twelve. Two for each house.

[*The woman has watched his performance with growing bewilderment. At the end of it she tries to cope with the situation with another laugh. Pause. The man, under pressure, tries again, now more desperately.*]

Miss Frieda Joubert! There's no water left. . . .

WOMAN. I know.

MAN. There's no water left in Bontrug. Dam's empty.

WOMAN. I know! You told me.

MAN. Little mud left for the goats. They're going to start bringing in for us on Monday. We've got to be ready with our buckets at twelve. Two for each. . . .

WOMAN. You've already told me!! Don't you remember . . . ?

[*Her desperation now growing. A move to him. He backs away from it. He is hanging on.*]

MAN. Miss Frieda Joubert. There's no water left in. . . .

WOMAN. Why are you . . . ?

MAN. There's no water left in Bontrug!

WOMAN. What are you doing?

[*Her bewilderment now edged by anxiety. Equivalently his performance degenerates more and more.*]

MAN. Please listen, Miss Frieda! There's no water left in Bontrug, man. Dam's empty. Little mud left. For the goats. They're going to start bringing in for us. . . .

WOMAN [*her desperation mounting*]. You've already said that!

MAN. Miss Frieda . . . they going to start bring for us. . . .

WOMAN [*hanging on to herself*]. And I said . . . I said I'd send you some of mine and you. . . .

MAN. I got to be ready with my buckets at twelve.

WOMAN. You got angry!

MAN. Two buckets, lady. Got to be ready with my buckets at twelve. 'Cause they sending to us . . . me and my buckets . . . two for each. . . .

[*The woman now starts to lose control. The man's 'performance' has now degenerated into a grotesque parody of the servile, cringing 'Coloured'.*]

WOMAN. Sit down!

MAN. Bontrug's dry. Little mud in the dam.

WOMAN. Come!

MAN. Water, Miesies. Please, Miesies . . . water. . . .

WOMAN. The way you. . . .

MAN. Just a little. . . . We're thirsty . . . please, Miesies. . . .

[*The woman, now almost hysterical, looks around wildly for an affirmative action.*]

WOMAN. Sit down . . . here . . . and read. . . .

MAN. Water, Miesies, water, Miesies.

WOMAN. No, no . . . stop it . . . [*knocking the hat out of his hand.*] STOP IT!

MAN. I'll . . . I'll just go. I'll use the back door.

[*Camera flashes and finally torches as in the previous sequence. This time, however, the torches trap the man against a wall and the woman on the floor looking down at the man's jumbled pile of clothing. To start with she is completely unaware of the torch shining on her.*]

WOMAN. I don't understand. . . . You can't. Don't even try. [*Carefully examines one of his shoes.*] Dust on his shoes. Him. His feet. His thoughts. A man . . . walking, from Bontrug to here, the town, to me . . . and then back again. [*Pause.*] One night I watched him through the window, walk away, quietly, quickly, and disappear down the street. I tried to imagine. . . . [*Pause.*] I can't. [*Very carefully replaces the shoe as she found it. His clothes. She is trying hard to understand.*] There is no water in Bontrug! . . . I'm not thirsty. . . . I don't understand. . . . He uses the back door. He can't come to me any other way. When I heard the knock and opened it, the first time, wondering who it was . . . and saw him. . . . No! I didn't. I saw a coloured man. . . . I was not surprised. Because it was the back door.

MAN. I needed a book. I knew I couldn't be a subscriber. But it was my third assignment. . . .

WOMAN. . . . Julian Huxley's . . . *Principles of Evolution*. . . .

MAN. . . . and I didn't have any of the books on their list. It had happened with the first two as well.

[*Both talk to the torches, and each other, in a frank and eager manner.*]

WOMAN. He was very serious about it. Explained what he was doing.

MAN. You were interested, hey.

WOMAN. Oh yes! Very. I could see it was important to him. I didn't have any of the books he mentioned . . . but I knew what he wanted and I found something else that I thought would help him. I said if there was anything I could do to help he must just tell me.

MAN. I could see she really meant it. So I didn't worry too much about going back again.

WOMAN. He always used my office. It started to seem so silly. Nobody was reading the books he needed. Only a few people ever went to that side of the library.

MAN. It made a big difference . . . being able to go there and use the encyclopedias, and read.

WOMAN. I found myself seeing books and articles in newspapers which I thought would help him. He's a very fast reader . . . and shy . . . at first . . . but once we started talking it was almost hard to keep up with him. And exciting. For me too. Even going home after I'd closed the library began to be different. I had something to do, and think about at night. You see, the library is not very busy . . . there's not all that much to look after.

MAN. We talked about lots of things, didn't we?

WOMAN. Oh yes! Not just the course. That's how we came to know each other. [*Pause as they both wait innocently and eagerly for a response to what they have said. Nothing. The silence slowly becomes a threat.*] Say something. [*Mounting hysteria.*] SAY SOMETHING! . . . Yes, we have made love. I switched off the light. Yes. Yes. Guilty. No doubt about it. Guilty of taking my chance and finding him. Hands, eyes, ears, nose, tongue . . . totally guilty. Nothing is innocent.

MAN. *Ja*, she put off the light. I mean . . . suppose I had made a mistake. Hey? And she wasn't feeling the way I did. Or even thinking about it. You know what I'm saying? I couldn't move. Just sat there looking at what I was thinking, and I couldn't move. It wasn't the first time I realized what was happening to us. We knew all right what we were doing. But that night I knew, it can happen now! If I was right about her, and did the right thing, it was going to happen. But suppose I was wrong. Suppose she screamed.

[*Camera flashes and finally torches as in the previous sequences. This time the torches trap the woman alone, naked. Once again she is unaware of the light shining on her. She studies herself, quietly, privately.*]

WOMAN. Ugly feet. The soles have got hard patches. My legs are bandy. Good calf muscles . . . probably got them riding to school on my bicycle up a very steep hill each day. Skin around my knees is just starting to get a little slack. I enjoy making the muscles in my thighs move. Hair is very mousy . . . very sparse. . . . I think the area around my waist is quite nice. Few soft and feminine contours around my hips.

My breasts are slacker than I would like them to be. My neck is unattractive. My face is quite interesting but can be very plain sometimes. Lines around my mouth are starting to worry me. Hair causes me concern. I think it's going off. Ashamed of my hands. Nail-polish has come off in patches. Skin looks very old.

I think there is a lot of me in my hands somehow.

My favourite colour is blue. . . .

My favourite flower is. . . .

You say you have no previous experience of men. That you were a virgin, and yet you took the initiative. What would you have done if Philander had rejected you?

Hated him.

Would the fact that a coloured man had rejected you have humiliated you more than if a white man had done so?

By the time it happened his colour did not mean anything to me any more.

Did you encourage Philander?

Yes.

Why?

I wanted him.

Would you say that you encouraged him against his will?

No. I think that he felt almost as strongly about me as I did about him.

Did it ever occur to you that he might have accepted a physical relationship with you out of respect for your feelings?

Yes. It did occur to me sometimes.

You are older than Philander?

Yes.

By how many years?

Six.

Do you think it possible that Philander thought you provided him with an easy opportunity to have intercourse with a white woman? Because as a Coloured man the law forbids it.

No.

What makes you so sure?

He was a man who had too strong a feeling of responsibility towards his family to take that chance for that reason.

Did you feel any responsibilities towards his family?

I did think about them for a time.

After you put out the light did he then initiate the physical encounter?

No.

What did you do. Describe what happened until you are told to stop.

I . . . I put off the light. . . .

Well. . . .

Yes . . . *ja* . . . I stood there. . . . I knew why I had put off the light. . . . But once I had put it off . . . I was . . . hesitant . . . I was nervous . . . I wasn't sure what to do next. . . . Well . . . he . . . he didn't move or do or say anything. . . . I knew it was so hard for him that if I didn't do something . . . nothing would happen . . . so I. . . .

[*Pause.*]

I knew where he was. . . . So I took a few . . . paces . . . towards him. . . . My hand came in contact with his . . . coat or jacket. . . . There was another moment of hesitation. . . . I had found him. And then. . . .

[*Pause.*]

I moved in close to him. I knew that the response coming from him was the same. I wouldn't have had the courage if I didn't know that he felt . . . that he. . . . So I leant against him . . . his shoulder. . . .

[*Pause.*]

He put his arms around me. . . . It felt like he . . . there was . . . his lips . . . yes. Then his lips touched the top of my head . . . it's very hard to remember anything.

[*Pause.*]

I know that we finally did kiss each other. Please, do I have to . . . please, it's very hard for me.

[*Pause.*]

So . . . so then . . . yes. . . . So then we made love. . . . I don't know how . . . but we were on the floor . . . the floor of the library. . . . And he. . . . And me. . . . We. . . .

[*Another sequence of flashes during which the woman scrambles round looking for the man and finally finds him—standing against a wall, protecting his genitals with his hands. This time the sequence does not end with torches, but harsh, directionless, white light. The image is suggestive of one of the photographs handed in in the Court as evidence and it is with this as a background that the policeman finally completes his statement.*]

MAN. There was nothing left to say. I had thought there would be. That if it ever happened, and we had known it could, that there would be something left to say, to her, to myself. Something to say to them. But when the light went on, it burnt out all the words I had left. Nothing to say. Nothing to do.

[*The policeman, still carrying his dossier and notebook, enters and completes his statement.*]

POLICEMAN. Exhibit A. We gained entry to the room by forcing the door, and put on the light. By this time Joubert had covered herself with a blanket. Exhibit B. I immediately arrested them, and asked them whether they wished to make a statement warning them, at the same time, that anything they said would be taken down in writing and could be used in evidence against them. Full stop. Joubert's response to this was: quote 'I'm not ashamed of myself' unquote. I asked her if she was prepared to repeat the statement in front of a magistrate. She said quote 'Anyone' unquote. She then turned to Philander and said quote 'I'm sorry' unquote. Philander said nothing. On being searched a key was found in Philander's trouser pocket. I asked him to identify it, and he said it was a key to the back door of the library. When I asked him where he had got it, he did not reply. Joubert then interrupted and said quote 'I gave it to him' unquote. The key is attached to the statement as exhibit C. I finally asked them to get dressed and to accompany me to the police station, where they were formally charged.
Signed: Detective Sergeant J. du Preez . . . South African Police. Noupoort.

[*Exit. A short pause and then the man leaves the pool of light*

*in which he and the woman had been standing. The woman is
totally isolated in her last speech, as will also be the case with
the man.*]

WOMAN. I am here. You are not here. I know that without
even trying to find you, as I did once, because nothing can
be here except me. That doesn't mean I don't want you. But
you are gone from other places. The pain will come. I'm
holding it far away. But just now I will have to let it go and
it will come. It will not take any time to find me. Because
it's mine. That pain is going to be me. I don't want to see
myself. But I know that will also happen. I must be my hands
again, my eyes, my ears . . . all of me but now without you.
All of me that found you must now lose you. My hands still
have the sweat of your body on them, but I'll have to wash
them . . . sometime. If I don't, they will. Nothing can stop me
losing that little bit of you. In every corner of being myself
there is a little of you left and now I must start to lose it. I
must be very still, because if I do anything, except think
nothing, it will all start to happen, I won't be able to
stop it.

MAN. Frieda! [*He discovers himself alone . . . with his clothes.*]
Now I must understand it.

If they take away your eyes you can't see.
If they take away your tongue you can't taste.
If they take away your hands you can't feel.
If they take away your nose you can't smell.
If they take away your ears you can't hear.
I can see.
I can taste.
I can feel.
I can smell.
I can hear.
I can't love.

I must understand it.
If they take away your legs you can't walk.
If they take away your arms you can't work.
If they take away your head you can't think.
I can walk.

I can work.
I can think.
I can't love.

I must understand it.
When you are hungry you eat.
When you are thirsty you drink.
When you are tired you sleep.
I will eat.
I will drink.
I will sleep.
I won't love.

I must understand it again.
If they take away your soul, you can't go to Heaven.
I can go to Heaven.
I can't love.

And then I'm running away very fast, from everything but
especially God, because he mustn't know. But the street doesn't
work any more. Because when I reach the end where the stones
and the darkness should start, the light goes on, and I come
out of the back door of the library and I've got to start running
again. But I can't run very fast. My hands get in the way
because I don't want them to see. So I'm crawling instead and
she is not surprised. Nobody is surprised. They still greet me.
But I know you see.
An arm without a hand.
A leg without a foot.
A head without a body.
A man without his name.
And I'm terribly frightened they will find out. That the dogs
will tell them. Because they can see. And then I'm sitting
just past the lamp-post where my shadow always turn into
the night and she asks me, 'What do you want?'
I don't know.
Yes, you do.
Everything.
You can't have it. Choose.
I can't.

You're a coward.

I know.

You realize it's useless.

Yes.

What will you do if they find out about us?

I don't know. So she tells me.

Nothing. You do nothing. They do it all.

Trust them. They know what to do.

They find you.

They put on the light.

They take the picture.

They take your name.

And then they take you.

And then they take your belt and your tie and your shoe-laces.

They lock the door.

They will ask the questions.

They will try you.

And then at the end as at the beginning, they will find you again.

Guilty.

That frightens me. I get up and I start running. And I can't understand why she doesn't call me back, because I'm only running home.

And then I'm in Bontrug. And the dogs don't bark at me, they laugh. They're all standing up and walking around on their back legs to show me theirs.

And then I reach my house. But I don't find anyone there, only God, waiting in the dark. And now I'm too tired to run away any more. I just think he must have driven there by car because otherwise how could he have got there before me. He lives in the town.

And it's a court case. That on the night of January the twelfth 1966, I . . . who had been made in his image . . . did lose a part of me. They did it I say. They dug a hole and buried it. Ask the dogs. And then Frieda comes in to give evidence. It's very dark. God shines a torch to see what she looks like. Did he have it, he asks her. Yes, she says. Then he asks me: 'Why did you let them do it?'

So I tell God I don't smoke and I don't drink and I know the price of bread. But he says it makes no difference and that he wants back what is left. And then I start to give him the other parts. I give him my feet and my legs, I give him my head and body, I give him my arms, until at last there is nothing left, just my hands, and they are empty. But he takes them back too. And then there is only the emptiness left. But he doesn't want that. Because it's me. It's all that is left of me.

They arrest it all the same.

Now I'm here.

There is nothing here.

They can't interfere with God any more.

THE END

GLOSSARY

ag voetsek: go to hell
bioscope: cinema
brak: mongrel dog
broer: brother
Ciskei (*adj.* Ciskeian):   one of the Black 'homelands' created by the South African Government under its policy of Separate Development
dankie: thank you
gqokra izi khuselo zamehlo kule ndawo: put on safety glasses here
hai; haai: exclamation of surprise
hier is ek: here I am
ja: yes
kieries: fighting-sticks carried by young African men
lap; lappie: rag
makulu: grandmother
meester: schoolmaster
moer: literally, womb; used as a swear-word equivalent to 'fuck', 'fucking'
nyana we sizwe: brother of the land
ons was gemoer vandag: we were fucked up today
poes: cunt
pondok: shack, shanty
spruit: spring, stream
tshotsholoza kulezondawo, nyabaleka: opening phrase of an African work-chant; literally, work steady, the train is coming
tsotsis: **Black hooligans**